Cromosys Publication

Teach Yourself Adobe After Effects

NIRANJAN JHA SHOWMAN

Founder - Niranjan Jha Showman

Education and Technology Research Center

Patankar Park, Nallasopara (W), Mumbai. +91-9561450045

Education, Technology, Publication, Healthcare, Newsmedia, Realtor, Filmmaking

www.facebook.com/cromosys

+91-9561450045
Learn Advanced Skills
And Get Job Instantly
GERMAN
Python
FRENCH
C++
SPANISH
Java
ENGLISH
HTML5
RUSSIAN
CSS
JavaScript
Cromosys
Education and Technology Research Center
Nallasopara (W), Mumbai

Learn Web Programming
Demo-Class Free
HTML
CSS
React
JavaScript
Typescript
Bootstrap
Cromosys
20 Years of Experience
Nallasopara (W), Mumbai
+91-9561450045

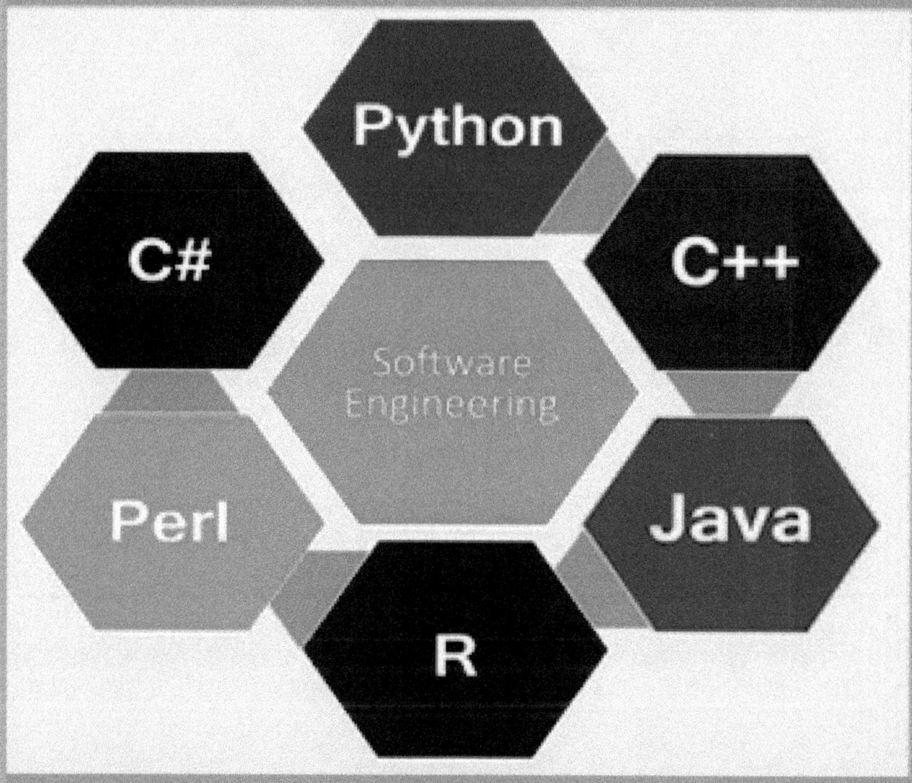

+91-9561450045
Learn Software Engineering
Demo-Class Free
Python
C#
C++
Software
Engineering
Perl
Java
R
Cromosys
20 Years of Experience
Nallasopara (W), Mumbai
+91-9561450045

25 Years of Experience
Learn Visual Multimedia

Animation VFX
Movie Editing
Game Development

Cromosys
+91-9561450045
Education and Technology Research Center
Nallasopara (W), Mumbai
www.facebook.com/cromosys

Jobs Available
For Candidates Who Know

German
French
Spanish

Vacancy in Germany, France, Spain

For Hospitality, Engineering, IT Sector
With Free Visa, Airfare and Accommodation

Cromosys
Education and Technology Research Centre
Nallasopara (W), Mumbai
+91-9561450045
20 Years of Experience

+91-9561450045

Foreign Languages Institute

German, French, Spanish

Basic and Advanced - All Levels
3 x 6 = 18 Courses

FRANCHISE
Business Offer

Teaching Materials Provided
We have 1 Million Students Globally
Great Income Assured
Global Exposure

Cromosys
20 Years of Experience
Nallasopara (W), Mumbai
+91-9561450045

Book: Teach Yourself Adobe After Effects
Author: Niranjan Jha Showman
Publisher: Cromosys Publication
ISBN: Acquired
Date: 2020
Category: Computer Education

Preface

Cromosys Publication's **Teach Yourself Adobe After Effects** book is an optimal quality guide to the beginners and advanced learners. We are the leading book publisher of languages and technology. Our research and education center working for last fifteen years has made tremendous efforts to simplify the learning of After Effects, and so we assure you that this book will walk you through in the simplest way in your entire course of learning, and will make you a master of this application in just one month of time. This book provides an in-depth and systematic introduction of After Effects, and explains the key concepts of video graphics. Using After Effects, you can create your own engaging motion graphics with new and improved techniques, such as 3D camera tracker, ray-traced 3D renderer, global performance cache, new bevel and extrude properties, and Mask Feather Tool. This book also explains the methods such as cropping, color correction, and retouching and healing images and how to use layers to edit images nondestructively. Distinguishing features of the book are it follows a step-by-step approach, supplemented with practical examples, and real-life screenshots. Being simple, precise, and complete, this book empowers you to get started with opening After Effects to creating professional visual effects for movies and Web publishing. With the lessons offering the readers a cutting edge in After Effects CS6 and the latest version by providing step-by-step procedures and multiple illustrations, this book has become an ultimate reference that you can use anytime and anywhere. This manual is covered in such a way that it will be equally helpful to the novice users as well as the professionals. The tutorials conceived and prepared by us will let you start learning from real basic making your move amazing, astonishing, and exhilarating for you. It's cool, simple, and sublime!

Niranjan Showman, the author of this and fifty other books published online, is the coiner, founder, and owner of Cromosys Corporation. His dedication in technological and linguistic research is significantly known to millions of people around the world. This book is the creation of his avowed determination to make the learning of After Effects CS6 easy to the people. After you install the application on your system, you just have to follow the instructions of this book doing the same on your computer, and you will see that you are quickly learning everything. Just an hour of practice per day, and in a month of time you'll get a lot of knowledge, tips and tricks to work with this software. This is an unmatchable unique book of its kind that guarantees your success. The lessons are magnificently powerful to bring you into the arena of cinematic visual effects. With the industrial growth from the year 2014, the accurate and profound knowledge of this software has influenced millions of minds; therefore we conceived the idea of making this book a guideline for those who want to be perfect in this application starting from real basic. What After Effects does, no other software can do. It is the need of time that is why many people have been sharpening their knowledge to be good in it.

After Effects is an industry-standard application used for animation and compositing. It is primarily used in the post production stage of film and television production. It is closely integrated with Premiere Pro, Photoshop, and Illustrator to deliver superior quality motion graphics. Using After Effects, you can animate, manipulate, and compose different media types including images, ext, video, and audio in two-dimensional (2D) and three-dimensional (3D) spaces. You will find various built-in tools or third party plug-ins with which you can enhance a video and create professional visual effects. For instance, using Clone Stamp Tool, you can remove a portion of a video shot. In addition, you can optimize a source video to focus on key elements using the color correction effects.

Cromosys, our education and technology research center, saving human efforts from being wasted, is committed to help you gain profound and contemporary knowledge. The world growing with density has brought enormous opportunity to visual-effects talents irrespective of their geographical boundaries. We strongly believe that this book is useful for people working for graphics and animation, media houses, and entertainment world. After you start the lesson, you don't need to worry about anything but just follow each and every step carefully. This book is designed to fulfill the instant need of learners in a very economical way, as it is easy to find on Internet and affordable to buy and share. Cromosys, our path-breaking pioneer training institute for Computer Courses, English Speaking, Mass Communication, Foreign Languages, and Competition Coaching, is dedicated to enlightening human mind with educational endeavors, and we are doing the same for last successful fifteen years. And recently we have come up with 'Worldwide Online Teaching System' for languages and technology. We not only hope but believe that your success is in your hand, as this book will take you miles ahead in your expectation. We always respect the views and comments of readers, so for any communication with regards to assistance, enquiry or collaboration, we are always there at your reach as it helps us improve our quality.

Niranjan Jha Showman
Founder: Cromosys Corporation
Web: facebook.com/cromosys
Contact no.   +91-9561450045
Email address: cromosys@yahoo.com
Nallasopara (W), Mumbai, India

Books by the same author:
Teach Yourself Autodesk Maya, Teach Yourself Autodesk Combustion, Teach Yourself Autodesk 3ds Max, Teach Yourself Adobe Flash, Teach Yourself Adobe Dreamweaver, Teach Yourself Tally, English Voice Accent and Pronunciation, English Word Power, English Dictionary of Modern Slang, Teach Yourself Spanish, Teach Yourself French, Teach Yourself German, Teach Yourself Chinese Language Mandarin, Teach Yourself Japanese

Cromosys
Education and Technology Research Center
Education, Technology, Publication, Healthcare, Realtor, Filmmaking
Nallasopara (W), Mumbai, India

Caution: All the writing works that include all the educational, non-educational books, novels, and articles of the author Niranjan Jha, are the registered contents of Online Digital Services and also published contents of his registered magazine FACE OFF - Inventing Truth, which carries registration no. MAHENG12112/13/1/2009-TC and the endorsement no. 3244 28/5/2009 with the Ministry of Information and Broadcasting, Govt. of India. Any plagiarism in this regard will attract strict legal action. Any further publication of any of his books requires his written permission. Copyright certificate of this book is attached at the end of this book.

Lesson 1
Introduction

In this book, you will learn about the new and improved features of After Effects. The tutorial will help you create projects and compositions by importing, previewing, trimming, and looping footage items. You will get an explanation of the shape tools, such as Star Tool and Pen Tool used to create vector shapes. You will also learn the methods to create interesting path effects using Path Operations, such as Repeater and Zig Zag. While starting animation, you will learn to create and animate a brush stroke. You will also get acquainted to the new 3D camera track feature that is used to extract camera motion as well as 3D scene data by analyzing a video sequence. While animating, you will learn about keyframe animation technique where it explains how to animate layer transformations by adding keyframes over time. This book will also introduce the procedure to create the typewriter effect and to work with 2D and 3D text and animate them using animation presets. The advanced steps, such as creating masks and modifying them, including the new Mask Feather Tool will also be taught to you. You will get a description on using track mattes and chroma keys to remove blue and green screens that you use to create special effects. At the end, you will learn the procedure to add and modify audio, light, and camera and render the final composition in various formats.

With the introduction of global performance cache, After Effects now utilizes full computer resources improving the workflow significantly. The graphics pipeline of After Effects CS6 draws onscreen images using both OpenGL and video card. While working with compositions of larger image formats, After Effects CS6 provides fast manipulation of layers with graphical overlays, such as masks, motion tracker points, and bounding box handles. The new edition also includes features, such as Global Performance Cache, new Bevel and Extrude properties, new material options, 3D camera tracker, ray-traced 3D renderer, Mask Feather Tool and new 32-bit effects.

Understanding Motion Graphics

Motion graphics are basically the computer generated graphics which are used to create an illusion of movements in a video. Using the animation and video technologies, you can create an illusion of motion. To enhance the overall quality of an image, a presentation, or a story, you can integrate motion graphics into various mediums, such as film and television. Recently, After Effects has emerged as a popular choice amongst several video professionals for creating visually engaging motion graphics. Digital displays, such as high-definition (HD) televisions, monitors, and projectors, have enhanced the display of motion graphics. Earlier, motion graphics was created for standard definition (SD) video; currently, it is mostly created for HD videos. Let's learn about few of the frequently used terms while working with motion graphics.

Digital Video

There are two types of video: analog and digital. Analog video represents video signals using continuous signals of red, green, and blue. Digital video represents video signals as a sequence of digital data or in binary format. You can create digital video using a series of digital images displayed in quick succession. The advantages of using digital video include ease of sharing and storage of data without degradation of data quality when transferred to any other storage device. Moreover, digital video is inexpensive as compared to analog video. Regardless of the platform for which you are creating digital video content, you will come across terms, such as pixel dimension, frame rate, pixel aspect ratio, frame aspect ratio, resolution, and transparency.

Pixel Dimension

Pixels are the smallest components in a digital image, either a still image or a video frame. Now when we talk about pixel dimension, it refers to the number of pixels present in the width (horizontal) and height (vertical) of a video frame. For instance, in pixel dimension 1280x720, the first number represents the horizontal value and the second number represents the vertical value.

Frame Rate

Frame rate refers to the number of individual frames or images that make up each second of a video. Frame rate is measured in frames per second (fps). Different video standards have different frame rates. For instance, the National Television Systems Committee (NTSC) standard uses a frame rate of 29.97 fps and the Phase Alternating Line (PAL) standard uses a frame rate of 25 fps.

Pixel Aspect Ratio and Frame Aspect Ratio

Pixel aspect ratio refers to the ratio of height to width of a single pixel in an image or video frame. This ratio varies in display devices such as television and monitors. Frame aspect ratio refers to the ratio of width to height, such as 4:3 in the dimensions of a video frame. In a frame aspect ratio of 4:3, 4 refer to width and 3 refer to the height of an image or a video frame, respectively. There is also a widescreen frame with a frame aspect ratio of 16:9.

Resolution and Transparency

With regard to an image, resolution is the number of pixels in a given space measured in pixels per inch (ppi). It represents the pixel density of an image. However, in case of video, resolution refers to the pixel dimensions of a video frame; it represents the number of horizontal and vertical pixels, which make up the actual image. A higher resolution has more number of pixels per square unit of an image; a lower resolution has fewer numbers of pixels per square unit of the image. In general, standard resolution for images created for printing high quality graphics is usually 300 ppi; whereas, the default resolution for the Web or onscreen graphics is 72 ppi.

Video graphics are created using the red, green, and blue (RGB) color mode. In each frame of a video graphic, every individual pixel is assigned a unique color value consisting of combinations of the three primary colors, red, green, and blue. Certain video graphics are created using the RGBA color mode, where A represents the alpha channel. In After Effects, the term alpha channel refers to the transparency of an image or a video file. Alpha channels use 256 shades of gray to represent transparency, where black pixels represent fully transparent areas, white pixels are fully opaque, and gray pixels represent semi-transparent areas. Commonly used file formats that support alpha channel are Tagged Image File Format (TIFF), QuickTime Movie (MOV), Portable Network Graphic (PNG), and Flash Video (FLV). Alpha channels are automatically created for the transparent areas of native Photoshop and Illustrator files while importing them into After Effects.

Exploring the New and Enhanced Features

After Effects CS6 has several new features, such as new material options, environment layer support, and extrusion and bevel for shape and text layers. It is major release with the introduction of the global performance cache 3D camera tracker, Mask Feather Tool, and ray-traced 3D renderer. The global performance cache is the combination of disk cache and other performance enhancements.

To understand the basic as well as advanced functionalities of After Effects CS6, we will discuss the new and enhanced features of it the following list:

Global Performance Cache: Improves the After Effects CS6 workflow and makes it more responsive by utilizing full power of the computer hardware. This feature also provides real-time results while working with memory intensive features, such as 3D and previewing. The global performance cache consists of features, namely: global random access memory (RAM) cache, persistent disk cache, cache work area in background, and faster graphic pipeline. These features efficiently utilize the available RAM, hard disk space, video card, and 64-bit central processing unit (CPU) cores on a computer.

3D Camera Tracker: Extracts camera motion and 3D scene data by analyzing a video sequence. It helps to effectively integrate 3D objects into a 2D scene. You can choose Animation> Track Camera or Effect> Perspective> 3D Camera Tracker from the Menu bar to analyze footage and extract camera motion. The extraction process is analyzed and solved in the background. After completion of the process, small colored x's appear on the footage called 3D solved track points to place the 3D objects into the scene.

Ray-traced 3D Renderer: Refers to the enhanced advanced section and allows rendering enhanced 3D capability. You can render compositions in a separate environment from the existing Advanced 3D composition renderer, which is now called Classic 3D. Existing capabilities, such as soft shadows, motion blur, and depth-of-field blur are available in the new Ray-traced 3D renderer. New options include beveled and extruded text and shape layers, bending of footage and composition layers, environment map support, and additional material options.

New Bevel and Extrude Properties: Allows you to apply bevel or extrude on the 3D text and shape layers. Using properties such as Bevel Style, Bevel Depth, and Extrusion Depth you can modify beveled and extruded text and shape layers.

Bendable Footage and Composition Layers: Allows you to bend 3D footage and nested compositions around a vertical axis using controls such as Curvature and Segments in Geometry Options. Curvature is the amount of bend measured in percentage. Segments refer to the smoothness of the bend.

Environment Layer Support: Allows you to use 3D footage or nested compositions as a spherically mapped environment around a scene, visible on reflective objects.

New Material Options: Includes additional material properties, which affect the interaction of 3D objects with light. For instance, you can use reflection, transparency, and index of refraction as materials properties.

Fast Preview: Supports previewing in different levels of quality. This menu button has been reordered from highest quality and slower performance to lowest quality and faster performance. Few options have been renamed and the keyboard shortcuts assigned to them.

Mask Feather Tool: Allows you to refine a mask by defining points along it. Mask Feather Tool is present as a hidden tool under Pen Tool on the Tools panel. By default, pressing the G key toggles between Pen Tool and Mask Feather Tool. However, to toggle between all the tools under Pen Tool by pressing the G key, ensure that the Pen Tool Shortcut Toggles Between Pen and Mask Feather Tool check box is unchecked in the Preferences dialog box.

Layer Bounding Box and Selection Indicators: Displays layer bounding boxes and selection indicators on beveled, extruded, or curved layers. You can scale and rotate a 3D layer by manipulating the bounding box.

Rolling Shutter Repair Effect: Fixes footage containing rolling shutter distortion, which occurs mainly in digital cameras when the subject or the camera moves.

New 32-bit Effects: Includes 32-bit effects, such as Drop Shadow, Fill, Iris Wipe, Linear Wipe, Photo Filter, Radial Wipe, Set Matte, Spill Suppressor, and Time warp.

Understanding System Requirements

To install the After Effects CS6 application on a computer, you must verify if the computer is equipped with the essential system requirements to install and use the application. The system requirements include the operating system (OS), the Web browsers, and system hardware. It is important to know that After Effects CS6 requires 64-bit OS. The application cannot be installed on removable flash storage devices.

The installation of the application is a simple process. You need to insert the After Effects CS6 installer disc into the DVD drive. You may also download and use the free 30 days trial version of the software available at http://www.adobe.com/, and double-click the setup program and follow the onscreen instructions. To run After Effects CS6 on Windows operating system, you need the following system requirements:

- Intel Core 2 Duo or AMD Phenom ll processor
- 64-bit OS
- Microsoft Windows 7 with Service Pack 1
- 4GB or RAM (Adobe recommends 8GB)
- 3GB of free hard-disk space for installation and additional disk space for disk cache
- 1280x900 display
- OpenGL 2.0 graphics card
- DVD-ROM drive
- QuickTime 7.6.6
- Broadband Internet connection

OpenGL delivers high performance for graphic applications, such as Premiere Pro, 3ds Max, Maya, Combustion, and After Effects. It accelerates various types of rendering including screen for previews rendering.

Launching After Effects CS6

After you install the application, you can launch After Effects CS6 from the Start menu. If you launch a trial version, a dialog box appears with options to activate the product. Perform the following steps to launch the After Effects CS6 application:

1. Select **Start> All Programs> Adobe Master Collection CS6> Adobe After Effects CS6** from the Start menu. It opens the Adobe After Effects CS6 splash screen.

As you can see on your monitor, the splash screen displays the name and version of the application. After few seconds, the Welcome to Adobe After Effects screen appears. This welcome screen contains links to open projects, create a new composition, use help and support, and browse files using Bridge. The Recent Projects section lists the recently opened files; however, when you open the application for the first time, the Recent Projects section appears blank. You can also find links such as Getting Started, New Features, and Help using which, you can learn more about After Effects CS6. This welcome screen appears every time you launch After Effects CS6. In the welcome screen, you can select Show Welcome and Tip of the Day at startup check box to hide the screen during the launch of the application.

2. Click the **Close** button in the Welcome to Adobe After Effects screen. The Close button is at the bottom right side.

The default After Effects **application window** (also referred as interface) appears on your screen where you can create projects and compositions. This application window is shown in the picture 1.1 below. You can see in this picture that the After Effects CS6 application window includes several individual panels and panel groups. Using these panels, you can create motion graphics in After Effects.

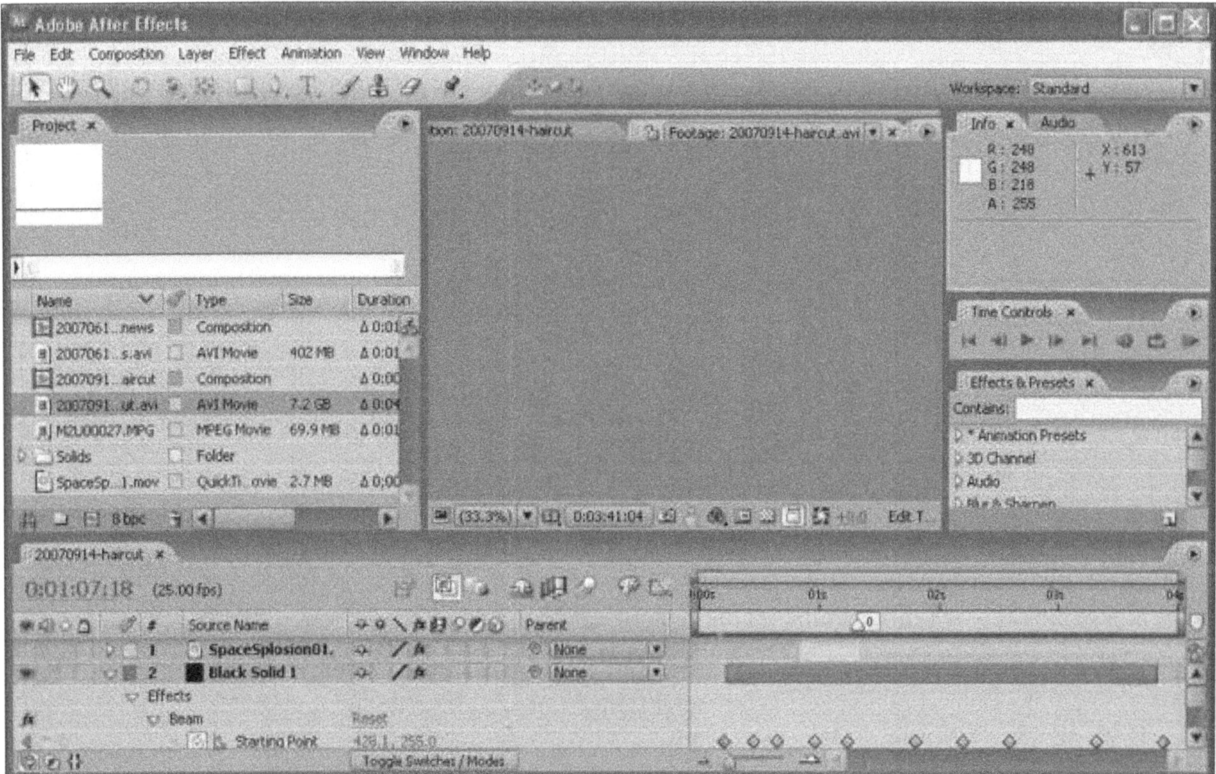

Picture 1.1

Exploring the After Effects Application Window

To provide a consistent user experience, Adobe has maintained a uniform look of the user interface across different audio and video applications, such as Audition, Premiere Pro, and After Effects. By default, each application displays its own set of panels; however, you can rearrange these panels similarly across all other applications. For instance, you can move and group panels by dragging them in each application.

The main window that appears when you launch After Effects is called the application window. This window consists of various panels organized in a specific format called workspace. By default, the Standard workspace is selected when you launch the application for the first time. The Standard workspace includes various panels, such as Project, Composition, Effects & Presets, and Timeline; and panel groups, such as Info and Audio. Using the application window, you can import various media files, namely: still images, video, and audio, and work with them using the combinations of tools and menu commands. The picture 1.2 shows the application window with various panels.

Picture 1.2

Let's now discuss few of the important and frequently used application window elements individually, starting with the Menu bar.

The Menu Bar

The Menu bar is placed under the Title bar of the After Effects application window. It contains nine menus, namely; File, Edit, Composition, Layer, Effect, Animation, View, Window, and Help. To access a menu command, click the respective menu, and then select the command from the dropdown list.

The Tools Panel

The Tools panel appears under the Menu bar in the application window. As soon as you create a composition, the tools in the Tools panel become available. After Effects includes tools such as Selection Tool and Hand Tool that enable you to modify elements of a composition. These tools are grouped based on their functionalities. To select a tool, click the respective tool icon on the Tools panel or press the assigned shortcut key on the keyboard. The Tools panel also displays the Workspace dropdown list and the Search Help text box. Using the Workspace dropdown list, you can select, create, delete, and reset a workspace. Using the Search Help text box, you can search help content in After Effects CS6. Let's learn now about the guidelines that help you to efficiently use the Tools panel:

- A tooltip appears when you hover the mouse-pointer over a tool icon. It displays the name and the keyboard shortcut of a tool.
- Pressing the assigned keyboard shortcut for a tool activates that tool. For instance, pressing the H key on the keyboard activates Hand Tool.
- A small triangle in the lower-right corner of the button indicates that there are one or more hidden tools.
- To select a hidden tool, click and hold the tool icon, and then select it from the flyout.
- To display the Tools panel in a floating window, click the dotted lines at the start of the Tools panel.
- To dock the Tools panel back, drag it to a preferred position and release when a green bar appears.
- To change the pointer for Brush Tool to crosshair, press the Caps Lock key. To return to the standard cursor, press the Caps Lock key again.

The Project Panel

The Project panel is one of the important panels in the After Effects workspace. It contains reference to all the media files (video, audio, and images) and compositions that you import or create inside an After Effects project. These media files remain in their original location on the hard disk drive and a link to them is created. Any changes made to the original media files are automatically updated in the After Effects project, where a new preview is generated accordingly. However, if you move, rename, or delete the original media files, the references in the Project panel do not work.

As you can see in the Project panel of picture 1.2, a thumbnail preview along with other information, such as dimension, duration, and fps of the selected media file appears at the top-left corner of the Project panel. The panel also displays a search text box, using which you can search media files in the Project panel. At the bottom of the Project panel, there are several buttons that help to create a new folder and composition, interpret footage, and delete the selected project items.

The Composition Panel

The Composition panel is the main preview window and animation area in After Effects. It appears at the center of the After Effects application window and contains the composition frame and the pasteboard area. The composition frame is surrounded by the pasteboard area, which is used to place those layers which are not currently being used. Using this panel, you can manually modify the content of a composition, which is the framework for a movie. You will learn more about compositions later in this book. You can create, show, or hide guidelines in the Composition panel. The alpha channel of a composition can be isolated to enable you to see those areas that are transparent or opaque. You can also change the preview of a composition as preferred using the Resolution/Down Sample Factor popup menu.

The Timeline Panel

The Timeline panel is primarily used to create animations in After Effects. It lets you animate layer and effect properties, position layers in time duration, and change the layer blending modes. Each composition has its own independent Timeline panel or timeline. The default display of the Timeline panel is the layer bar mode, as shown in the picture 1.3.

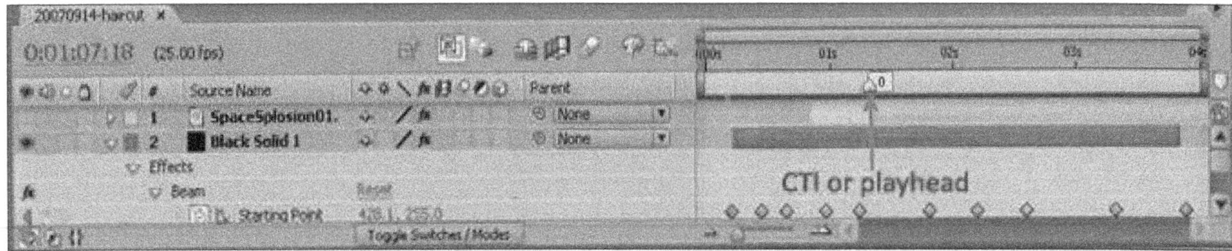

Picture 1.3

The Timeline panel displays the composition time as a time ruler across the top of the Time graph, while layer names and properties are displayed on the left. Current Time Indicator (CTI), also called the playhead, is the red vertical line that appears in the Time graph and runs perpendicular to the time ruler. It indicates the current frame that is being displayed as a composition or animation. In the next lesson, let's learn to create a new project.

Lesson 2
Creating a New Project

Professional artists use After Effects for animation, visual effects, and also for motion picture editing. Creating a project is the first step to create motion graphics in After Effects. A project in After Effects contains compositions and references to source files used in that particular project. After Effects does not store the copy of the source files inside the project file. Hence, you must always store the source files at the same location of the project files. You can only create and work with one project at a time in After Effects. If you create a new project with another project open, a message to close the existing project appears. Every time you launch After Effects, the program automatically creates a new blank project with the name, Untitled Project.aep*. The asterisk in the name indicates that the project has not been saved. To be on safer side, you can save the project which you are working on in your system hard drive.

Using the Project Settings dialog box, you can specify various project settings, such as Footage Start Time, Depth, Working Space, and Sample Rate. To open the Project Settings dialog box, select File> Project Settings from the Menu bar. Now let's go ahead and perform the following steps to create a new project in After Effects CS6:

1. Select **File> New> New Project** from the Menu bar in After Effects. It creates a blank project with the default name (Untitled Project.aep). After creating a project, you can specify its properties in the Project Settings dialog box.

2. Select **File> Project Settings** from the Menu bar. It opens the Project Settings dialog box, as shown in picture 1.4 below.

As you can see in the picture, you can configure the options available in the Time Display Style, Color Settings, and Audio Settings sections. In our case, we are using the same default settings without making any change in the Project Settings dialog box.

3. Click the **OK** button in the Project Settings dialog box. In the next section, let's learn to work with compositions.

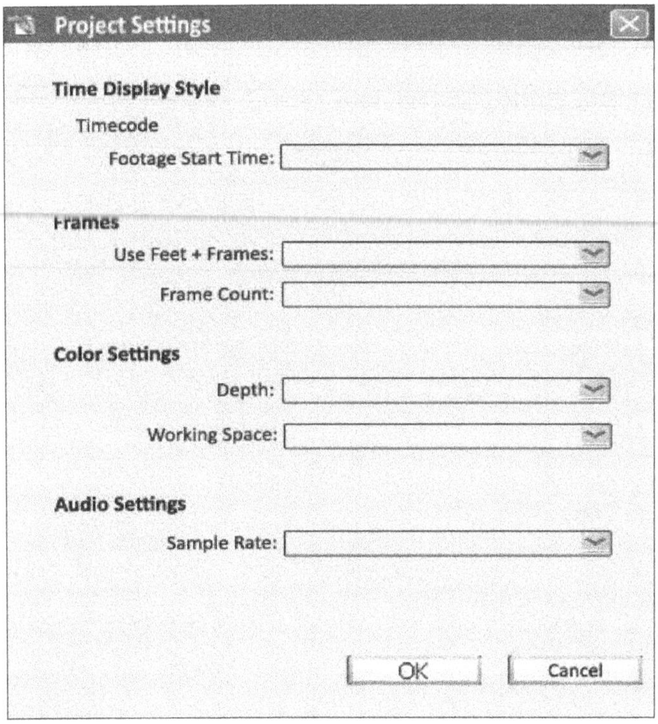

Picture 1.4

Working with Compositions

A composition is a framework for a simple or a complex project. Compositions are useful while working with large and complex projects. Within a single project, using compositions you can organize large amount of footage items and intricate effects sequence. A composition may include one or more layers. When you import footage items such as still image, video, audio, light, or camera into the Composition panel; it appears in a new layer. You can arrange the layers in a composition using the Composition or the Timeline panel. Each composition has its own timeline or Timeline panel. You can also create them inside another composition or import a composition into an existing one. Thus, you can organize the Timeline panel with hundreds of layers. Now let's learn about nested composition.

Understanding Nested Composition

When a composition is inside another composition, it becomes a nested composition. Nesting is the process of placing or nesting one composition inside another. You can also place multiple compositions inside other compositions. To create a nested composition, drag a composition inside the timeline of another composition. In the timeline, the composition appears as a layer, which can be edited by modifying its transform properties, such as Position, Scale, Rotation, and Opacity. Composition Navigator on the Composition panel displays the entire path of the nested composition. Arrows between composition names indicate the direction of the information flows, as shown in picture 1.5.

Picture 1.5

You can see in the picture 1.5 and the same on your computer screen that Composition Navigator is a bar above the Composition panel that shows the active composition in the same composition network. The compositions that appear in the Composition Navigator are the most recently active ones in the flow path of the currently active composition.

By default, the Flow to Left option is selected in the Composition panel menu. This setting is a global preference that applies to all compositions as well as to the Composition Mini-Flowchart view. You can show or hide Composition Navigator using the Show Composition Navigator option from the Composition panel menu, which is also created by default.

The Composition Mini-Flowchart is a temporary control that allows you to navigate within a composition network. You can click the arrow between the composition names to open the Composition Mini-Flowchart in Composition Navigator, as shown in picture 1.6. This picture shows the compositions immediately upstream (towards left) and downstream (towards right) of the selected composition. You can also click the Composition Mini-Flowchart button above the Timeline panel to display the composition flow path.

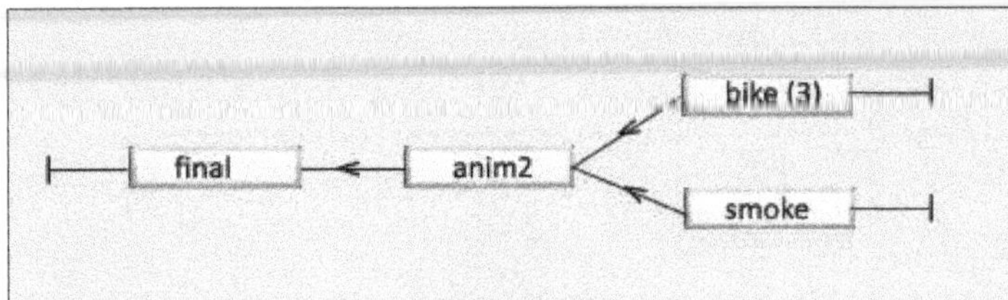

Picture 1.6

Creating a New Composition

There are various different methods that allow you to create a composition in After Effects. Using the Composition menu or the Project panel, you can create compositions by manually specifying the composition settings. To create a composition using Composition menu, you can select Composition> New Composition from the Menu bar. To create a composition using the Project panel, you can right-click an empty area and select the New Composition option from the context menu. In both cases, the Composition Settings dialog box appears where you can specify the required settings for the composition.

In addition, you can automatically configure settings such as frame size, frame rate, and pixel aspect ratio using presets. You can save the custom settings as a composition settings preset for future use. To do this, specify various composition settings values in the Composition Settings dialog box, and then click the Save button. To delete a composition settings preset, select it from the Preset dropdown list, and then click the Delete button. To restore the default preset, press the Save or Delete button while holding the Alt key down in the Composition Settings dialog box.

You can also change the composition settings after creating a composition. However, it is recommended to specify settings, such as frame aspect ratio and frame size, when you first create a composition. To modify the composition settings, you can select Composition> Composition Settings from the Menu bar. The Composition Settings dialog box displays the previously used settings. In After Effects, the composition duration limit is set to three hours and the maximum composition size is 30,000 x 30,000 pixels.

Now we can discuss about the methods to create compositions. Following are the methods that you can use to create compositions in After Effects:

- Select Composition> New Composition, or press the Ctrl+N keys together.
- Drag the footage item to the Create a new Composition button at the bottom of the Project panel.
- Select File> New Comp from the Selection from the Menu bar after selecting a footage item. In this case, composition settings including frame size (width and height) and pixel aspect ratio are automatically set to match the characteristics of the footage.
- Drag a footage item (still image, audio, or video) onto the Timeline panel. After Effects automatically creates a new composition with the same name as the footage item.
- Right-click in an empty area of the Project panel and select the New Composition option from the context menu.

To understand the instructions mentioned above, you need to perform the same on your computer. Let's do the following steps to create a new composition:

1. **Create** a new project or open an existing project in which you want to create a composition. In our case, we have created a new project with the default settings.

2. Select **Composition> New Composition** from the Menu bar. It opens the Composition Settings dialog box, as shown in picture 1.7.

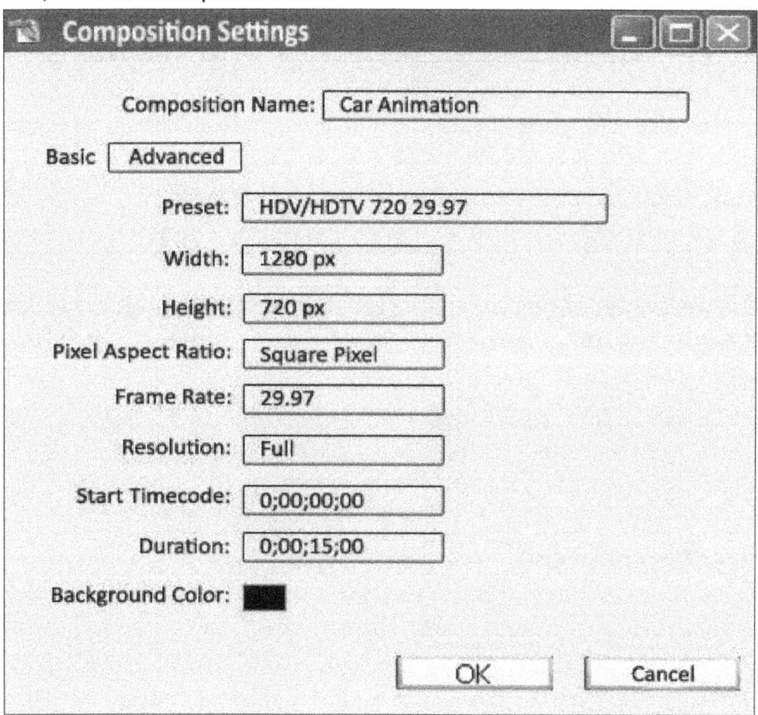

Picture 1.7

3. **Type** the name in the Composition Name text box as: **Car Animation**. Then **select** the composition settings preset from the Preset dropdown list as: **HDV/HDTV 720 29.97**. In this preset, the Width is set to 1280 px and Height is set to 720 px. In addition, the Frame Rate option is set to 29.97.

4. **Type** time duration for the composition in the <u>Duration</u> text box as: **0;00;15;00** or 15 seconds. Then **select** the composition <u>background color</u> as **Medium Gray-Royal Blue**.

When you click the color swatch, the Background Color dialog box opens, where you can select a preferred composition background color. To pick a color, select the hue from the vertical color slider, and then click in the color field. Alternatively, you can type the numeric values that represent a color.

5. Click the **OK** button at the end to create a composition with the specified settings. The Car Animation composition is added to the current project, which appears in the <u>Project panel</u> of the After Effects screen.

If you look at the After Effects screen on your monitor, you will notice that the Composition panel also displays the new composition in which the background color appears as Medium Gray-Royal Blue, as defined in the Composition Settings dialog box. In case you want to change the composition settings after creating a composition, you can right-click the composition in the Project panel and select the Composition Settings option from the context menu. It opens the Composition Settings dialog box. Following are the important settings available in the Composition Settings dialog box:

Composition Name: Allows you to specify a name for a new composition.
Preset: Allows you to select the built-in composition settings from a dropdown list. You can use these presets to create compositions for Web, film, and television productions. Two buttons appear to the right of the menu: Save and Delete. The Save button lets you save custom presets and the Delete button lets you delete presets.
Width: Specifies the width of a composition, which is measured in pixels.
Height: Specifies the height of a composition, which is measured in pixels.
Pixel Aspect Ratio: Specifies the shape of the pixels in a composition. An incorrect pixel aspect ratio can distort a composition.
Frame Rate: Specifies the number of frames displayed per second for a composition.
Resolution: Specifies the quality of the Composition panel display. Lower resolution requires less RAM to preview a composition.
Start Timecode: Specifies the frame of a composition or beginning of the timeline. The default timecode of a composition is 00;00;00;00. This value does not affect rendering.
Duration: Specifies the duration of a composition in the timeline.
Background Color: Allows you to select a composition background color. The default color is black. The eyedropper next to the color swatch allows you to pick colors.

Importing Photoshop/Illustrator Files as Compositions

Adobe Photoshop and Illustrator are two industry-leading applications for creating raster (pixel-based) and vector (mathematically defined functions) graphics, respectively. After Effects allows you to import native Photoshop or Illustrator file as a composition. The file that you want to import in After Effects from Photoshop or Illustrator may be an image consisting of a single layer or multiple layers. In After Effects, there is flexibility to control the importing of layered Photoshop and Illustrator files as single layered footage or convert into a new composition with multiple layers. If you import a file as footage, the layers are automatically flattened. Flattened file is similar to a still image, which is imported in After Effects. When you import a layered Photoshop or Illustrator file as a composition, the layered structure is maintained and the individual layers are not flattened.

You can select File> Import> File (or Multiple Files) from the Menu bar to import footage into After Effects. Additionally, you can import footage using Adobe Bridge, which is powerful and flexible way to import footage items. Perform these steps to import Photoshop or Illustrator file as a new composition:

1. Select **File> Import> Multiple Files** from the Menu bar. It opens the <u>Import Multiple Files</u> dialog box on the screen.

2. **Navigate** to a folder location of the file in the Look in dropdown list and **select** the (.psd) Photoshop file. Then click the **Open** button of the Import Multiple Files dialog box. It opens the Photoshop file's dialog box with the import options.

3. Select the **Composition – Retain Layer Sizes** option from the <u>Import Kind</u> dropdown list. By default, the Footage option is selected in the Import Kind dropdown list.

4. Click the **OK** button at the bottom. The selected Photoshop file appears as a composition in the Project panel and the Import Multiple Files dialog box reopens.

5. Navigate and **select** the (.ai) Illustrator file that you want to import. Then click the **Open** button, which opens the dialog box of the selected file.

6. Select the **Composition** option from the <u>Import Kind</u> dropdown list. The Layer Options section is disabled when you select the Composition option.

7. Click the **OK** button at the bottom. The selected Illustrator file appears as a composition in the Project panel and the Import Multiple Files dialog box reopens.

8. Click the **Done** button to close the <u>Import Multiple Files</u> dialog box. Now you can see the two imported compositions in the Project panel.

As you can see in the Project panel of your screen, there are two folders created automatically along with the compositions. These folders contain individual layers for Photoshop and Illustrator files. By default, the folders are collapsed. You can click the arrow besides the folder icon to expand them. The number of layers imported into After Effects depends on the number of layers in the native Photoshop or Illustrator file. Any sub-layers under a layer are flattened with the parent layer and imported as one layer. You can now use the individual layers and animate them separately in the Timeline and Composition panels. In the next lesson, let's learn about saving a project in After Effects CS6.

Lesson 3
Saving a Project
After creating a project and compositions, and then importing footage items for building a project in After Effects, the next important step is to assign a meaningful name to the project for saving it. While saving the project, you can use the Increment and Save command to specify the version of the project file to enable opening in earlier versions of After Effects as well as other applications, such as Premiere Pro. The Increment and Save command keeps track of the versions of the saved file. You can use this function to maintain previous versions and update the project file. Perform the following steps to save the project that we have created and modified in the previous lessons:

1. Select **File> Save As** from the Menu bar to open the <u>Save As</u> dialog box. Then **navigate** to the folder in which you want to save the project. In our case, we select the folder named **Used Resources**.

2. **Type** a name in the <u>File name </u>combo box. In our case, we type **Blank Project**. Then click the **Save** button in the Save As dialog box.

By default, After Effects saves the project in its native format, which is Adobe After Effects Project (*.aep). The native format is selected in the Save as type dropdown list.

Customizing After Effects CS6

Customization allows you to modify the application as required. There are several ways to customize After Effects CS6 such as changing the appearances (workspace brightness) of the interface and the default undo-level. You can also create a custom workspace by arranging and positioning all the panels in the interface and saving it for later use. In addition, you can enable the Auto-Save feature to enable saving the project at regular intervals. After Effects includes several predefined workspaces, such as Standard, Animation, Effects, Text, and Motion Tracking. Each workspace includes relevant panels that are used frequently. For instance, the Paint workspace displays the panels required to work with the paint tools. The default workspace Standard includes the Tools, Composition, Project, Effects and Presets, and Timeline panels. Let's learn to customize a workspace in After Effects CS6.

Customizing a Workspace

Customizing a workspace allows you to show only those panels required for working on a project. You can customize a workspace by arranging the panels in the layout that best suits your working style for specific tasks. You can drag the panels to new locations, move them into or out of a group, place them alongside each other, and undock a panel to float it in a new window. As you rearrange panels, the other panels automatically resize to fit the window.

To move a panel, drag its tab to another location. The location over which you move the panel becomes highlighted, which is known as a drop zone. The drop zone determines the insertion of a panel into a workspace. If you drop a panel along the edge of another panel or group, it docks next to the existing panel group. It resizes all the panel groups to accommodate the new panel. In addition, if you drop a panel in the middle of another panel or panel group, or along the tab area of a panel, it adds to the existing panel group and places at the top of the stacking order. You can also use the panel menu icon located at the upper right corner of each panel to customize it. After making changes to the position or layout of panels, you can save the workspace with a preferred name for future use. Perform the following steps to customize a workspace by displaying, relocating, and removing panels from the default workspace:

1. **Ensure** After Effects is running with the **Standard** workspace selected. To do so, look at the option selected that says **Standard** beside the <u>Workspace</u> tab, which is shown in picture 1.8 in a red rectangular box at the top right corner of the screen.

2. Select **Window> Align** from the Menu bar to display the <u>Align panel</u>. The Align panel appears on the application window at the bottom right side of the screen, as shown in picture 1.8 with the red arrow numbered 2.

3. **Click** and **drag** the Info panel tab (shown in picture with red arrow numbered 1) over any preferred location. In our case, we move the Info panel over the Project panel (red arrow 3). Then **release** the mouse button to place the Info panel as a separate panel over the Project panel.

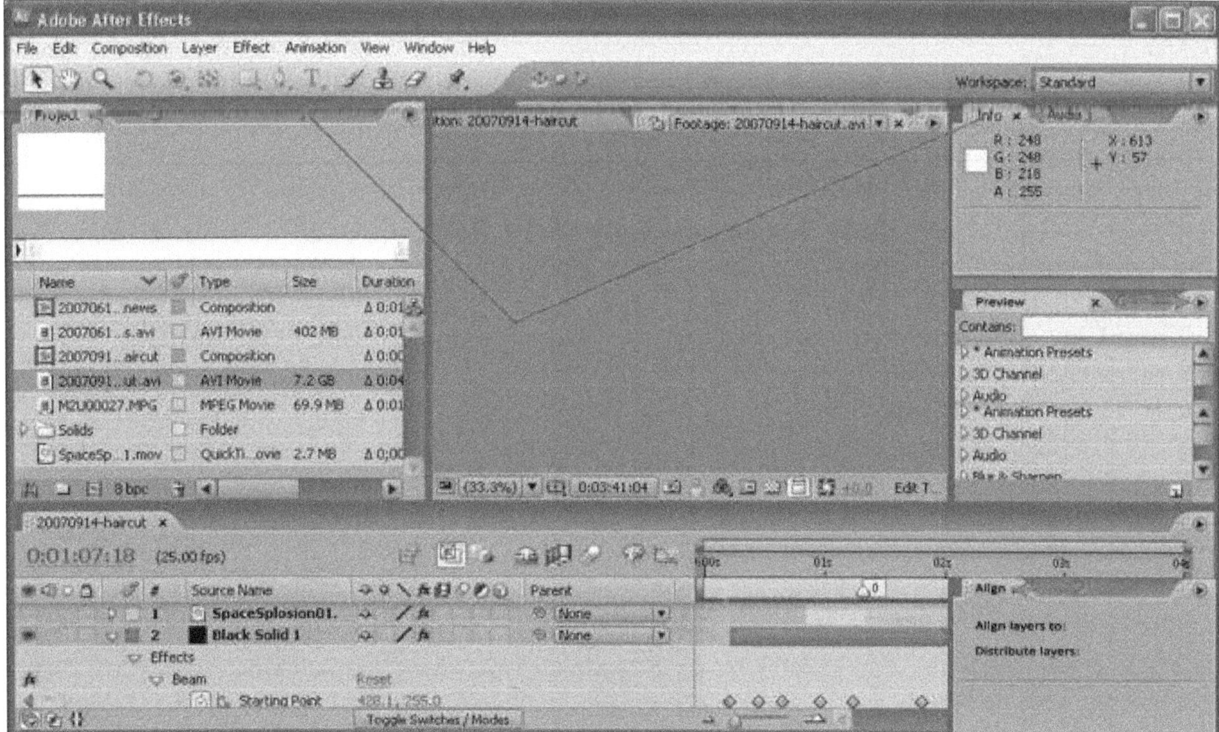

Picture 1.8

4. **Click** the panel menu icon of the Preview panel (shown in picture 1.8 with red arrow numbered 4). It opens a panel menu on the screen.

5. Select the **Close Panel** option from the panel menu. The Preview panel disappears from the workspace. Now that we have customized the workspace, we need to save it as a custom workspace.

Saving a Workspace

Saving a custom workspace is as important as customizing a workspace. You can save a custom workspace along with a project in After Effects. After customizing a workspace, you can save it as a new workspace with a specific name. The name of the new workspace appears in the Window> Workspace submenu and in the Workspace dropdown list on the Tools panel. If a project with a custom workspace is opened on a system other than the one on which it was created, After Effects searches for a workspace with a matching name. In case, After Effects cannot find a matching name, it uses the current local workspace to open the project. Perform these steps to save the previously customized workspace:

1. **Open** the previously customized workspace, and **click** the Workspace dropdown list, which is shown in picture 1.8 in a red rectangular box at the top right corner of the screen.

2. From the dropdown list, select the **New Workspace** option to open the New Workspace dialog box. Then click the **OK** button in the dialog box.

The Workspace dropdown list on the Tools panel displays the new workspace. Using the Workspace dropdown list, you can reset or delete a workspace. For instance, by selecting the Reset "Standard" option from the dropdown list, you can reset the Standard workspace to its original layout.

Changing the Workspace Brightness

In After Effects, you can change the brightness level of the application window. Changing the brightness affects the panels, dialog boxes, and windows. The default workspace brightness is set to medium dark. You can select darker or lighter color brightness for the application window. To change the color brightness, adjust the Brightness value in the Appearance category of the Preferences dialog box. Perform the following steps to change the workspace brightness:

1. Select **Edit> Preferences> Appearance** from the Menu bar. It opens the <u>Preferences</u> dialog box with the Appearance settings.

2. **Drag** the slider handle in the <u>Brightness</u> section to change the level of brightness. In our case, we change to lighter brightness level. Then click the **OK** button to accept the change. By the way, to change the default brightness level, click the Default button in the Brightness section.

Changing the Undo-Level

In After Effects, using the Undo command, you can go back to the previous steps to correct a mistake. You can go back one step at a time through several errors. By default, the undo-level is set to 32, allowing you to go back 32 times. However, you can modify the default settings using the Preferences dialog box. Higher number of undo-level gives you more steps to go back and rectify your mistakes, but consumes more memory. Perform the following steps to increase the undo-level:

1. Select **Edit> Preferences> General** from the Menu bar. It opens the <u>Preferences</u> dialog box with the General category.

2. **Click** the underlined text for the <u>Levels of Undo</u> option and **type** a preferred undo-level in the text box. In our case, we have typed: 50. Then click the **OK** button to save the change. By the way, the levels of undo depend on the amount of RAM available on your system.

Enabling the Auto-Save Feature

The Auto-Save feature automatically saves a copy of a project file as you work. It helps to avoid loss of work in case of a power failure or computer programs crash. It saves the After Effects project incrementally and at regular intervals at a specified location. The original file is not modified; instead, After Effects creates a copy of the original file. You can set the frequency of the Auto-Save feature to save a project and the number of copies of a project saved. By default, the Auto-Save option is set to 20 minutes and a maximum of five project versions. After Effects saves the project file in every 20 minutes. You can modify these settings as required. Perform the following steps on your system to enable the Auto-Save feature:

1. Select **Edit> Preferences> Auto-Save** from the Menu bar. It opens the <u>Preferences</u> dialog box with the Auto-Save category.

2. Enable (put check mark) the **Automatically Save Projects** check box. Then set the **Save Every** option to 10 Minutes.

3. Set the **Maximum Project Versions** option to 10. Then click the **OK** button on the right side of the dialog box.

By setting the Save Every option to 10 minutes, changes to a new project is saved every 10 minutes. Similarly, it saves up to ten versions of the project file as set in the Maximum Project Versions option. After saving ten project versions, it replaces the first Auto-Save version.

Quitting After Effects CS6

After the work session is complete, you can close the project and quit the application. Closing a project does not quit the application; it only closes the current project. You can close a project using the Close command under the File menu or by pressing the Ctrl+W keys on the keyboard together. To quit the application, you need to use the Exit command under the File menu or press the Ctrl+Q keys together.

Lesson 4
Working with Footage

After Effects is primarily used to modify, animate, and compose different media types including image, text, animation, video, and audio to create cinematic visual effects and motion graphics. When you start a new After Effects project, you must first import the media files (footage items) that you want to use in the project. There are different ways to import the footage items into an After Effects project. You can either use the Import command or the Project panel. Using the Import File and Import Multiple Files dialog boxes, you can select and import footage items from a single and various folders, respectively.

The project panel displays a thumbnail preview and other information, such as file type, dimension, and time duration above the panel. In the Project panel, the order of footage items does not affect the appearance of the composition unlike in the Timeline panel. After Effects also allows you to create and use folders to organize the footage items; preview them using the Footage panel; trim and loop video or audio footage items. Trimming allows you to hide the unnecessary portion in a project. Looping allows you to play a short audio or video clip repeatedly.

Overview of Projects, Compositions, and Layers

The three major frequently used terms in After Effects are projects, compositions, and layers. A project is the nucleus of all the work you do in After Effects; it stores references or links to all the media files used in a project. In simple terms, a project acts as a container storing references to each imported media file, instead of embedding the actual media files. As the media files are not embedded in the project file, it becomes dependent on imported media files. This referencing system helps in reducing the size of the project file. In addition, you can still modify imported media files in their native application, such as modifying a Photoshop document in Photoshop or editing a video in Premiere Pro. If the original files are modified, a new preview is generated in After Effects and its project is updated accordingly. If you move, rename, or delete the original media files, it causes problems, such as media files may disappear from the composition in the Composition panel. After Effects displays the missing file message and prompts to relocate the file each time you open the project.

A composition, also referred to as comp, is an individual container used to combine media files, apply effects, and renders the output. The term composition is derived from the word composite and is similar to a sequence in video editing application, such as Premiere Pro and Final Cut Pro. Each composition represents an independent timeline and can contain combination of videos, audios, still images, and other elements, such as shape layers, lights, and cameras. Every element used in a project is not external and imported into After Effects; elements, such as compositions, shapes, lights, and cameras, are created internally in After Effects and stored as part of the project file. A composition can also contain other compositions, which are referred to as nested composition. In After Effects, nested compositions help to create complex animations.

If you are familiar with graphics applications, such as Photoshop, Illustrator, or Flash, you must be familiar be concept of layer. Each media file in a composition is placed into its own track in the Timeline panel known as a layer. You cannot directly edit a media in a composition; instead, you must place them in layers. Each layer has properties, such as position, opacity, and duration, which you can adjust separately or with other layers. You can also add variety of effects to a layer using the Effect menu.

Importing Footage Items

To create motion graphics, the first step is to import different footage items into the Project panel. In After Effects, a footage item refers to the basic unit in a project. For instance, you can import different types of footage items, such as still image, image sequences, audio, video, and both single and multi-layered Photoshop/Illustrator files. You can also import After Effects and Premiere Pro projects as footage items. There are different ways to import footage into a project:

- Select File> Import> File or (press Ctrl+I) keys together to import files located in a single folder. It opens the Import File dialog box.
- Double-click the lower empty area of the Project panel to open the Import File dialog box.
- Select File> Import> Multiple Files to select files located in different folders. It opens the Import Multiple Files dialog box.
- Drag and drop the files from Windows Explorer into the Project panel.
- Use Adobe Bridge to search, preview, and import footage items in After Effects.

The Project panel acts as a container for footage items that you import into the After Effects as well as the footage items that you create in After Effects, such as compositions, shapes, lights, and cameras. It also provides information about footage items, such as Type, Size, Duration, and File Path. In the Project panel, the footage items are listed alphabetically by default; you can customize these footage items. For instance, you can click the heading of the Type column to reorder the panel content to place similar type objects adjacent to each other. By the way, you can press the Tilde (~) key on the keyboard to toggle between the full screen view and the normal view of the current active panel. You can also use Project panel to create folders, subfolders, and compositions. Let's now learn to create folders and subfolders.

Creating Folders and Subfolders

Folders are useful tools for organizing the content (footage items) in the Project panel. You can manage footage items efficiently using folders and subfolders. For instance, you can move all the still images into a folder and give the folder a suitable name that represents the images. Similarly, you can move footage items between corresponding layers. This reduces the clustering in the Project panel while working with the large and complex projects. Using the Create a new Folder button at the bottom of the Project panel, you can create a folder. You can also create a folder inside another folder, which is referred to as a subfolder. Perform the following steps to create a folder and a subfolder:

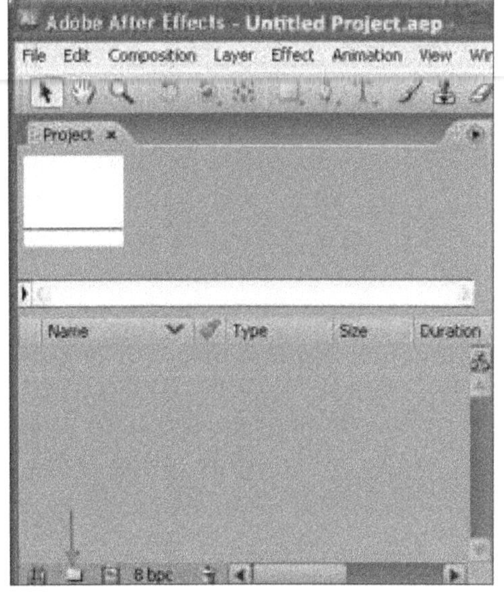

Picture 1.9

1. **Launch** After Effects CS6. By default, a new project is created naming Untitled Project.aep in the Title bar, as shown In picture 1.9.

2. Click the **Create a new Folder** button at the bottom of the Project panel, as shown in the picture 1.9 with the red arrow at the bottom. Alternatively, you can choose File> New> New Folder from the Menu bar. A new folder is created and the folder name (Untitled 1) is highlighted in a text box.

3. **Type** a name for the new folder in the text box. In our case, we type: **Car Animation**. Then press **Enter** key to accept the name. The Car Animation folder appears highlighted in the Project panel. By the way, to rename a folder, you can right-click the folder and select the Rename option from the context menu.

Similarly, you can create multiple folders in a project. In case, a folder is selected, you need to deselect it to create a new folder. If a folder is selected, clicking the Create a new Folder button creates a subfolder. Let's now proceed to create a subfolder under the Car Animation folder. In our case, the Car Animation folder is still selected.

4. Click the **Create a new Folder** button again. A subfolder is created and the default name (Untitled 1) is highlighted in a text box.

5. **Type** a name for the subfolder in the highlighted text box. In our case, we type: **Still Images**. Then press the **Enter** key or click an empty space to accept the name. The subfolder is named as Still Images and appears highlighted.

Likewise, you can create folders inside a subfolder, which is known as nested folder. You can click the arrow icons that appear besides the folder icons to expand and collapse the corresponding folders. By default, when a subfolder is created, the folder expands automatically. You can click the arrow to hide the content of the folder when it is expanded. Alternatively, to create a new folder, right-click an empty space of the Project panel and select the New Folder option form the context menu.

Importing Image Sequences

Image sequences are series of sequential images. For instance, a video clip of two seconds can contain 48 different sequential images. You can produce image sequences in applications such as Photoshop and Premiere Pro or using devices, such as scanners and digital cameras. The name begins with a file name followed by a number and then file extension; for instance, carrotTop0001.jpg. When you select an image in a sequence, After Effects searches for the other images with similar names in that folder. Perform the following steps to import an image sequence as a single entry:

1. **Select** a folder into which you want to import the image sequence, or **deselect** the selected folders if you do not want to place it in any folder. In our case, we have deselected all the folders.

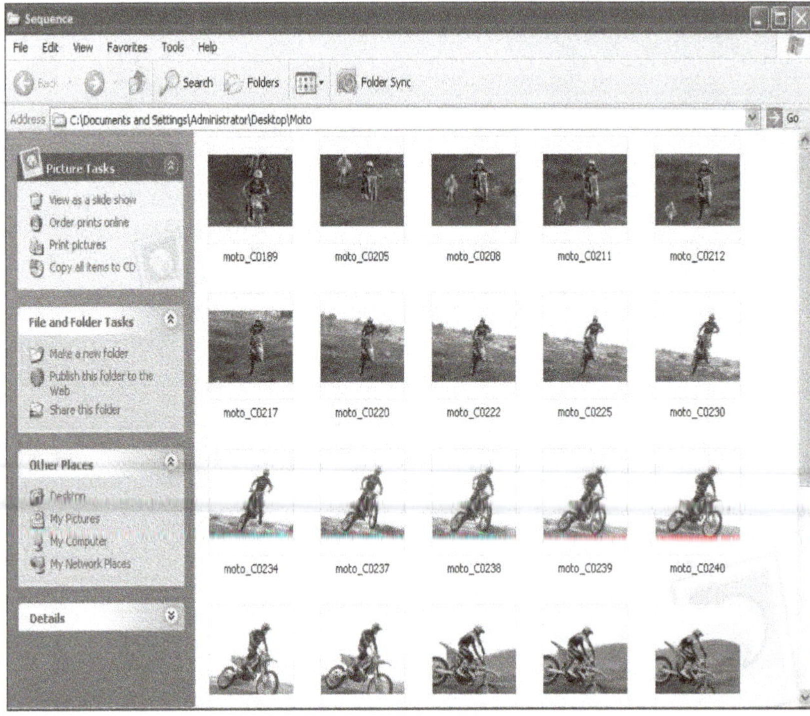

Picture 2.0

2. Select **File> Import> File** from the Menu bar to open the Import File dialog box. Then **navigate** to a folder in your hard drive which contains the image sequences. In our case, we select a folder named Sequence containing the image sequence.

The Image sequences are the cluster of still images in a folder, in which a second image shows a step advancement from the first image, and the third image shows a step advancement from the second image, and so on. The picture 2.0 shows the open view of our Sequence folder.

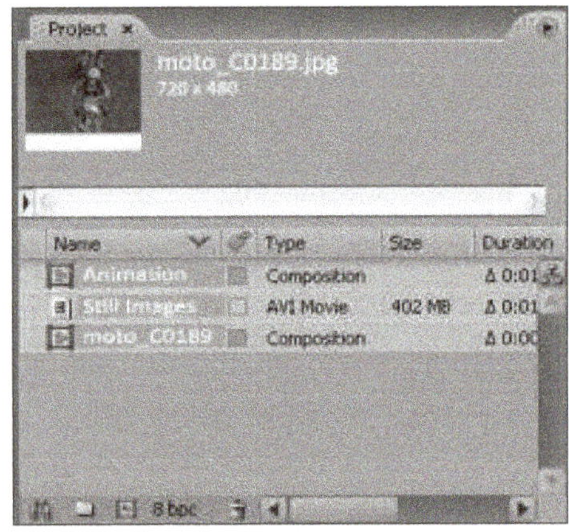

Picture 2.1

For instance, if you want to make a movie of a boy riding a bike in After Effects, you should have the cluster of still images of it each image advancing from the other. You can create this kind of images in Photoshop and Premiere Pro with a lot of patience.

3. **Click** the first image file in the folder. In our case, we select moto_C0189.jpg. Then click the **Open** button in the folder. The Image sequence is imported in the Project panel as a single entry named **moto_C0189.jpg**, as shown in picture 2.1. In the next section, let's learn to import still images, video, and audio files.

Importing Still Images, Video, and Audio Files

After Effects allows you to use wide variety of footage items including still images, video, and audio files into a project supporting standard formats, such as Tagged Image File Format (TIFF), Joint Photographic Experts Group (JPEG), Windows Media Video (WMV), Audio Video Interleaved (AVI), Audio Interchange File (AIF), and MP3 of still image, video, and audio files. To use these footage items, you must import them into an After Effect project. As said earlier, you can import footage items in different ways: using Import command or using the Project panel. Here are the steps to import still image, video, and audio:

1. Select **File> Import> Multiple Files** from the Menu bar to open the Import Multiple Files dialog box. Then **navigate** to the folder containing the still image that you want to import. In our case, we open the Sample Pictures folder.

2. **Select** the still image, and click the **Open** button. In our case, we select Tulip.jpg. If you want, you can hold the Shift key down and click one or more files to select them simultaneously.

The still image (Tulip.jpg) appears in the Project panel and the Import Multiple Files dialog box reappears. The Import> File command allows you to select multiple files simultaneously; however, all the files have to reside in the same folder. The Import> Multiple Files command allows you to import multiple images from different folders. In the latter case, the Import Multiple Files dialog box reopens after importing selected files from the folder. Let's proceed to import a video file.

3. **Navigate** to the folder containing the video file that you want to import. In our case, we open the Sample Videos folder. Then **select** a preferred video file. In our case, we select Wildlife.wmv file.

4. Click the **Open** button. The Wildlife.wmv video file appears in the Project panel and the Import Multiple Files dialog box reappears. Let's now proceed to import an audio file.

5. **Navigate** to the folder containing the audio file. Then **select** a preferred audio file, and click the **Open** button. The audio file also appears in the Project panel and the Import Multiple Files dialog box reappears. Now click the **Done** button to close the Import Multiple Files dialog box.

The Project panel shows the various imported files. Importing layered Photoshop/Illustrator files as footage automatically flattens the layers in the file. However, if you import the layered file as a composition, After Effects imports each layer in the file as an individual layer.

Importing Premiere Pro Project

After Effects is primarily used in the post production stage of film and television productions. It is closely integrated with other Adobe applications, such as Premiere Pro, Photoshop, and Illustrator to deliver superior quality motion graphics. Such integration allows you to import a Premiere Pro native project into After Effects. You can either import a single sequence or all sequence in the Premiere Pro project. Using File> Import> Adobe Premiere Pro Project from the Menu bar, you can import a Premiere Pro project. Perform the following steps to import a Premiere Pro project:

1. **Open** the After Effects project and choose **File> Import> Adobe Premiere Pro Project** from the Menu bar. It opens the Import Adobe Premiere Pro Project dialog box.

2. **Select** the Premiere Pro project that you want to import, and click the **Open** button to import. The Premiere Pro Importer dialog box appears; here, you can choose the sequences that you want to import. By the way, the native format for a Premiere Pro project is .prproj.

3. **Select** the sequence from the Select Sequence dropdown list. Then click the **OK** button. By the way, with the Import Audio option, you can choose to import the audio with the project. The imported sequence appears in the Project panel. You can see on your screen that the sequence is placed in a folder named after the imported project.

Moving Footage Items

While working with large projects containing hundreds of footage items, proper management of those footage items is essential. There are several methods that you can implement to organize footage items in the Project panel. One method can be placing similar footage items into separate folders or subfolders. For instance, you can place all still images in a separate folder or all footage items used for composition in a separate folder. To move footage items, create a folder or subfolder and then drag the footage item over the folder. Perform these steps to move a footage item:

1. In Project panel**, create** a folder or subfolder into which you want to place the footage items (shown in picture 1.9). You can **name** the created folder or subfolder as: **Still Photos**. In our case, we want to move still images into Still Photos subfolders.

2. In Project panel, **click** and **drag** the still image over the <u>Still Photos</u> subfolder. In our case, we drag Tulip.jpg over the Still Photos subfolder.

3. **Release** the mouse button to move the still image footage item into the Still Photos subfolder. By default, the still images appear hidden. To show the content of the folder, you need to expand it.

Lesson 5
Interpreting Footage Items

When you import a piece of footage (for instance, video), After Effects analyzes the footage using a set of rules to determine the source file attributes, such as pixel aspect ratio, alpha channel type, frame rate, and color profile. This information is used to determine the display of the footage. The Interpret Footage dialog box allows you to set these attributes manually. You can also modify these rules for all footage items by editing the interpretation rules file. The settings in the Interpret Footage dialog box vary based on the type of file and information contained in it. Typically, the interpretation settings determine the following:

- The interpretation about the interaction of the alpha channel with other channels
- The frame rate to be assumed for the footage item
- Whether to separate fields; if yes, the filed order to be assumed
- Whether to remove 3:2 or 24Pa pulldown
- The pixel aspect ratio of the footage item
- The color profile of the footage item

Now to understand it practically, you can perform the following steps on your computer to interpret a footage item:

1. **Select** a footage item in the <u>Project panel</u>. In our case, we select Wildlife.wmv video footage.

2. Click the **Interpret Footage** button at the bottom left of the Project panel, as shown in picture 2.2 with the red arrow. Alternatively, you can select File> Interpret Footage> Main from the Menu bar to open the Interpret Footage dialog box.

Picture 2.2

In the Interpret Footage dialog box of After Effects, you can configure various settings in the Main Options and Color Management tabs. By default, the Main Options tab is selected; you can configure settings in different sections, such as Alpha, Frame Rate, Start Timecode, Fields and Pulldown, and Other Options.

3. In the **Interpret Footage: Wildlife.wmv** dialog box, select the **Conform to frame rate** radio button. Then **type** the frame rate: 30. In After Effects, frame rate is measured in frames per second.

4. In the Loop text box, **type** the value: 2. Then you need to click the **OK** button at the bottom of the dialog box.

Alternatively, you can open the Interpret Footage dialog box by pressing the Ctrl+Alt+G keys. You need to highlight the footage item in the Project panel before pressing the keys.

Previewing Footage Items

You can preview a footage item using its native program before importing into After Effects. For instance, you can preview a Photoshop Document in its native program, Photoshop. You can also preview a footage item in After Effects after you import it. To preview a footage item, double-click on it in the Project panel. The footage item opens in the Footage panel for previewing. The Footage panel is not displayed by default; to display it, select Window> Footage: (none) from the Menu bar. This opens an empty Footage panel that is grouped with the Composition panel. If a footage item is previewed, the name of the footage item appears adjacent to the panel name in the Window menu. You can preview a still image, video, or audio using the Footage panel.

Previewing Still Images

The Footage panel allows you to preview still images in different formats, such as JPEG, TIFF, PNG, or BMP. You can double-click a still image in the Footage panel to preview it. The still image opens in the Footage panel, where you can preview by modifying some of the basic properties, such as zoom level, exposure, grid display, and region of interest. You can access the options at the bottom of the Composition panel. Following list describes the options used for previewing:

- Using the Magnification ratio popup dropdown list, you can change the zoom level.
- Using the Adjust Exposure property, you can modify the exposure of the footage item for preview only. Negative values subtract lights from the preview image; while positive values add lights to the preview image.
- Using Choose grid and guide options popup menu, you can display grids and guides.
- Using the Region of Interest property, you can focus on specific region of an image.

Now to understand it practically, you can perform the following steps on your computer to preview a still image using the Footage panel:

1. In the Project panel, **double-click** the name of the still image footage item to display it in the Footage item. In our case, we double-click the Penguins.jpg still image. It opens the Penguins.jpg footage item in the Footage panel on your screen.

In the Footage panel of your screen, you can see the text on the tab changes to Footage: Penguins.jpg. At the bottom of the Footage panel, several options appear; for instance, you can select a different magnification level from the Magnification ratio popup dropdown list. By default, the magnification level is set to 50%.

2. In the Footage panel, **select** another magnification level from the Magnification ratio popup dropdown list. This list is at the bottom left side of the Footage panel. In our case, we select 100%. As the result, the footage item magnifies to 100% level.

3. Click the **Adjust Exposure** property in the Footage panel. This option is at the bottom right side of the Footage panel. It opens a temporary text box. Then **type** the value: 10 in the text box. As the result, the adjusted exposure value is displayed.

To reset the exposure setting, click the Reset Exposure button. Similarly, you can use other properties, such as Region of Interest for previewing. You can drag a region to highlight an area. This displays the area outside the rectangular region in block, enabling you to focus on the area inside the rectangular region. After dragging the region, you can later modify the dimension of the rectangular shape. You can also move the rectangular shape from one position to another. You can disable this property by clicking the Region of Interest button again.

Previewing Video

Similar to previewing a still image, you can preview a video footage in the Footage panel. However, unlike a still image, the Footage panel for a video footage has a time ruler that helps you to adjust the time duration. Double-click the video footage in the Project panel to open the preview in the Footage panel. The Take Snapshot button in the Footage panel allows you to take snapshots and save it in the clipboard. Using the Show Snapshot button, you can later view the snapshot. Perform the following steps to preview a video footage item in the Footage panel:

1. **Double-click** the footage item in the Project panel. In our case, we double-click Cycle Animation.mp4 footage. It opens the selected video footage in the Footage panel on the screen.

At the bottom of the Footage panel several options appear, such as Magnification ratio popup dropdown list and Current Time button; using these buttons, you can change the zoom level and current time of the video footage item, respectively.

2. Click the **Current Time** button (which says: 0;00;00;00) at the bottom of the Footage panel. It opens the Go to Time dialog box on the screen.

3. Enter a new time duration: **0;00;04;00**, and click the **OK** button in the Go to Time dialog box. The Time Marker moves to the specified time duration and the Footage panel displays the video frame at 4 seconds.

You can also drag the Time Marker through the time ruler to move a video back and forward. This technique is called scrubbing and used to navigate quickly to a specific time in the file. When a video file is loaded into the Footage panel, press the Spacebar key to play the video and press the Spacebar again to stop the video.

The Current Time button at the bottom of the Footage panel indicates the time duration, also known as time code of the footage or video. This type of time display is used in video editing and motion graphics programs, such as Premiere Pro and After Effects. The time code consists of a series of four numbers separated by semicolons and provides an address to each frame of a video. The numbers represent Hours: Minutes: Seconds: Frames, starting from the left. The number of frames that make up a second depends on the composition settings. For instance, a video can be 30 frames per second (fps) for American Television Standard, 25 fps for European Standard, or 24 fps for film standards.

Previewing Audio

Similar to still image and video footage items, you can preview an audio using the Footage panel. You can import an audio file and double-click the file to load it into the Footage panel. However, you cannot play the audio by pressing the Spacebar key. You can use the random access memory (RAM) preview to preview an audio. The RAM preview allocates adequate RAM to play the audio, up to the frame rate of the composition. The RAM preview allows you to play footage in various panels, such as Layer and Footage. The amount of RAM available to the After Effects application determines the frame rate at which the audio is played. Perform the following steps to preview an audio using the RAM preview:

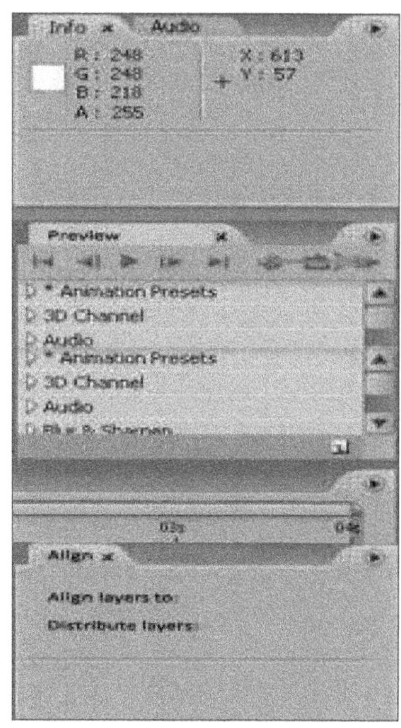

1. **Double-click** an audio footage item in the Project panel to load it into the Footage panel. In our case, we double-click Wildlife.mp3 audio footage. This footage item opens in the Footage panel.

2. Click the **RAM Preview** button in the Preview panel, as shown in the picture 2.3 with the red arrow. By the way, the Preview panel is displayed in the Standard workspace, which is selected by default.

Picture 2.3

As the result, the audio file begins to play. You can stop the playback by clicking anywhere in the interface or by pressing the Spacebar key. You can also use the playhead (Time Marker) to preview the audio file, by dragging it back and forth in the time ruler.

Trimming a Video Footage

Video clips often include extra portions at the beginning and end. These extra portions are referred to as handles. In addition, you might want to use only a small portion of a long video clip as required. The process of shortening a video clip is called trimming. Trimming hides the portion of the video clip instead of deleting. You can trim a video by adjusting its In Point and Out Point. The first frame of the footage is known as the In Point; whereas, the last frame of the footage is known as the Out Point. You can trim the footage by modifying its In Point and Out Point in the Footage, Layer, or Timeline panel. By trimming at the beginning or end of the footage, you can determine those frames to be first or last in the composition. Perform the following steps to trim a video footage using the Footage panel:

1. **Double-click** a video clip in the Project panel to load it onto the Footage panel. In our case, we double-click Rain 01.mp4 clip.

2. Click the **Current Time** button at the bottom of the Footage panel, (shown in picture 2.4 with the red arrow numbered 1). It opens the <u>Go to Time</u> dialog box. Then **type**: **5220** in the text box and **click** an empty area in the Go to Time dialog box. After Effects automatically converts the number to its time code equivalent. The number 5220 becomes 50 seconds and 20 frames (0;00;50;20).

3. Click the **OK** button in the Go to Time dialog box. The current Time Marker moves to the specified time duration in the Footage panel, (shown in picture 2.4 with the red arrow numbered 2).

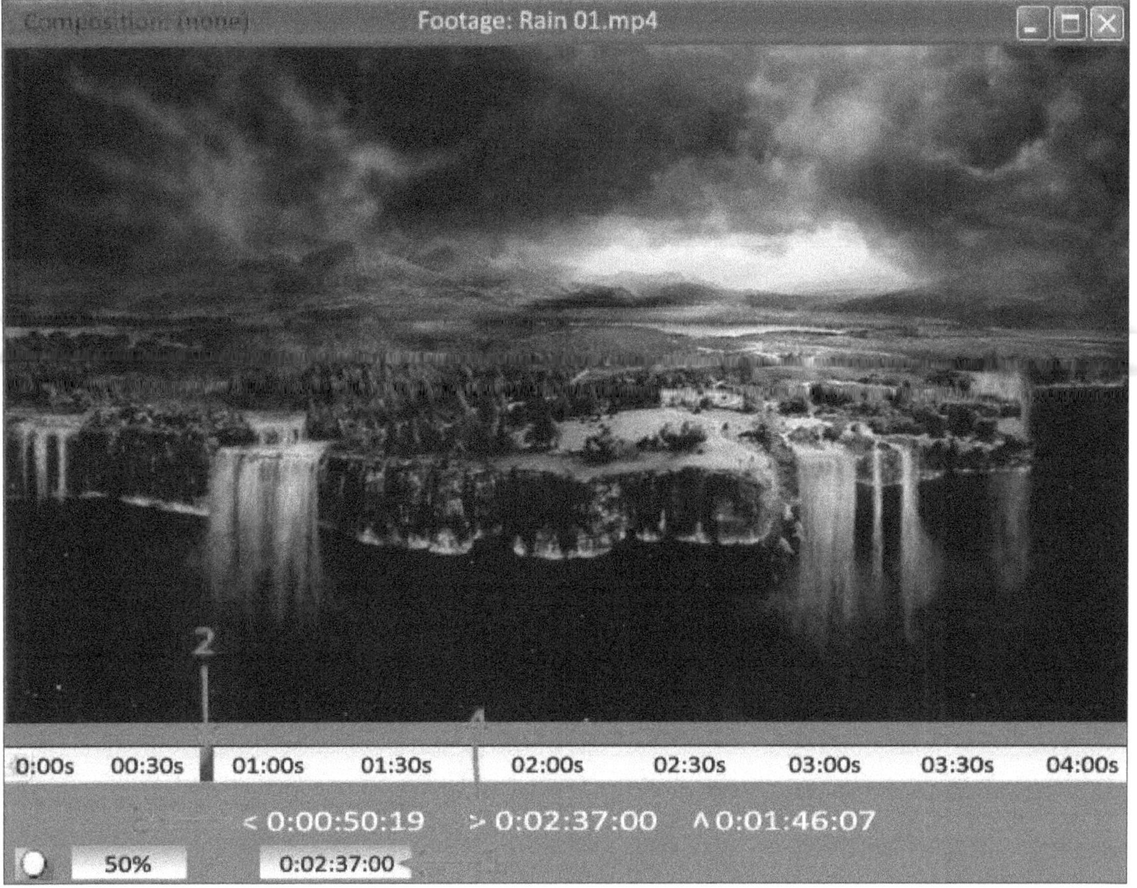

Picture 2.4

4. Click the **Set In** point to current time button in the Footage panel, (shown in picture 2.4 with the red arrow numbered 3). The start of the video clip moves to the current position of the playhead.

5. **Drag** the Time Marker to a new time duration. In our case, we set the new time duration as 2 minutes and 37 seconds (0;02;37;00). The playhead moves to the specified time duration in the Footage panel.

6. Click the **Set Out** point to current time button in the Footage panel, (shown in picture 2.4 with the red arrow numbered 4). This moves the end of the video clip to the current position of the playhead.

The trimming process of the video clip is complete. Now, you can add the trimmed clip to a composition in the Timeline panel using the Ripple Insert Edit and Overlay Edit buttons in the Footage panel. These two buttons are enabled when there is composition. Similarly, you can trim an audio clip using the In Point and Out Point. By the way, if you drag and drop footage onto the Timeline panel directly from the Project panel, the trimming that you have done on the video clip is ignored.

Looping a Footage Item

Looping enables you to play an audio or video footage item repeatedly. You can also specify the number of times you want the particular clip to play. At times, the duration of an audio or video clip is not as long as the composition; in such cases, you can loop it. By default, all the imported audio and video clips are set to loop only once. Using the Interpret Footage dialog box, you can set the looping of a video or audio clip in After Effects. Perform the following steps to loop a video footage item:

1. **Import** a video clip that you want to loop into the Project panel. In our case, we import TextAnimation.avi clip. You will see on your screen that the properties of the video clip appear above the Project panel. In our case, the duration of the video clip is 0;00;24;29, indicating it is 24 seconds and 29 frames in length.

2. Click the **Interpret Footage** button at the bottom of the Project panel, as shown in picture 2.2. The Interpret Footage: TextAnimation.avi dialog box appears.

3. **Type** a value in the Loop text box in the Other Options section. In our case, we **type**: 4, and click the **OK** button in the dialog box.

The Project panel displays the video clip properties with the new settings. The total duration of the video clip is now 0;01;39;28, which is four times of its previous duration.

Locating Missing Files

At times, you may want to move your projects from one computer to another; hence, you must also move the original footage items stored on your hard drive along with the project file. After Effects creates a link to the original files when you import it. The Project panel displays the link to the file. When you open a project, After Effects checks the media links to ensure that the files are in their original location. If a file at the original location is deleted, renamed, or moved, a problem occurs. In case After Effects does not find any of the original file, it displays a warning message. The warning message contains the number of missing files. To fix this problem, you must re-link the missing files or replace them with the original file. Perform the following steps to locate missing files:

1. **Open** an After Effects project with missing files. In our case, we open Importing Footage Items.aep project. After Effects message box appears indicating that two files are missing since last save of project.

2. Click the **OK** button in the After Effects message box to close it. The Importing Footage Items.aep project opens in the After Effects window. The Project panel displays the missing files by prefixing the color bar icon to the left of the footage item name.

3. **Right-click** the missing footage item and select **Replace Footage> File** from the context menu. It opens the Replace Footage File dialog box. Then **navigate** and **select** the footage item, and click the **Open** button in the dialog box.

If there are multiple missing footage items in the selected folder, the other file is automatically linked. In case the missing files are moved to various folders, you may have to repeat the process several times to locate all the missing files. The color bar icon besides the footage item name is now replaced by another icon that indicates the file is linked to the original file.

Lesson 6
Working with Layers

A layer is one image or footage item stacked one on top of another. It enables you to see through the transparent areas beneath a layer. In a composition, layers can be used separately to modify footage items, such as video, audio, and still image. You can also place compositions as layers. Using the Timeline, Composition, and Layer panel, you can work with layers and compositions. A composition can consist of a single layer or multiple layers. A layer is highly flexible, as you can modify it without altering the underlying layers. You can also separate individual elements of the motion graphics project. Moreover, you can convert a two-dimensional (2D) layer into a three-dimensional (3D) layer. 3D layers have additional properties that allow you to transform them in 3D. You can also create lights and cameras in After Effects.

Each layer has five Transform properties, namely: Anchor Point, Position, Scale, Rotation, and Opacity. You can use these properties to modify and animate a layer. For instance, the Position property allows you to move the layer content; the Opacity property makes the layer content partially visible. A 3D layer has several Material Options properties. In addition, you can add lights and cameras into the composition to add a sense of realism to it and view the composition in different angles. You can also modify the default light and camera settings; for instance, casting shadows or enabling depth of field, as required. In this chapter, you first learn to use layers. Next, you learn to set properties, blending modes, and layer styles of a layer. You also learn to work with 3D layers, lights, cameras, and 3D camera tracker.

Using Layers in After Effects CS6

Each footage item that you place in a composition resides on a separate layer in the Timeline panel. In After Effects, compositions are made up of layers; compositions might contain thousands of layers or only a single layer. You can composite multiple layers, apply video and audio effects onto a layer, and animate either the object in the layer or the effects applied on the layer. Each layer has its own properties that you can manipulate or animate independently to create motion graphics. When you modify the properties of a layer in the Timeline panel, the original source footage item remains unaffected. Hence, you can use the same footage item as a source for more than one layer. By default, modifying a layer does not affect other layers; however, you can link layers to modify them simultaneously.

By default, a new layer begins at the start of composition duration. However, you can also begin new layers at the current time specified by Current Time Indicator (CTI) or the playhead by deselecting the Create Layers at Composition Start Time check box in the General category of the Preferences dialog box. After adding a layer to a composition, the next step is to scale and position the layer to fit in the frame of the Composition panel. When you create a layer with a still image, the duration of the layer and the composition are the same. You can also change the duration of the layer by trimming the layer after creating it. Using the paint tools and tracking motion from the Layer panel, you can draw masks. The Layer panel shows you a layer in its original state; before any kind of transforms. For instance, even if the Opacity property of a layer is changed to 50%; the Layer panel shows the layer at 100%, which is the default opacity.

If you double-click a layer in the Timeline panel, it opens in the Layer panel. Only one layer viewer can be displayed at a time and any previously active layer viewers are hidden. The Layer panel appears in a separate tab in the Composition panel group. The layer viewer dropdown list above the Layer panel has a list of layers that you previously previewed; hence, you can select from this dropdown list to preview. Using this dropdown list, you can also create a new layer viewer, lock the existing layer viewer, or close layer viewers. The new layer viewer appears as a separate tab in the panel group. In the dropdown list, a tick mark appears before the active layer, as shown in picture 2.5.

Picture 2.5

Adding a Layer/Composition into the Timeline Panel

By default, when you double-click a footage item in the Project panel, its preview appears in the Footage panel. However, if you double-click a composition in the Project panel, it opens in the Composition panel as well as in the Timeline panel, where you can edit the composition. You can also drag and drop a composition or a footage item onto the Timeline panel and the Composition panel to modify it. However, there is a difference in dragging and dropping compositions into two different destinations or position. When you place a composition or footage directly onto the Timeline panel, it is always placed at the center of the Composition panel. If you place it directly into the Composition panel, the composition or footage item is placed where you drop it. If you double-click multiple compositions in the Project panel, they appear in separate tabs in the Timeline panel. Perform the following steps to add a composition onto the Timeline panel:

1. **Create** an After Effects project and **import** the footage items. After you import, you will have a list of footage items in the Project panel, as shown in picture 2.6 with the red arrow numbered 1.

2. **Click** and **drag** a footage item over the Timeline or Composition panel. In our case, we drag the **Bird.JPG** footage item over Timeline panel, as shown in picture 2.6 with the red arrow numbered 2. As you drag a footage item from the Project panel, it appears onscreen as a gray wireframe box.

3. **Release** the mouse button to place the Bird.JPG footage item. As the result, a new composition is created with the name Bird and appears in the Timeline and Composition panels. The Bird.JPG footage item appears as a layer in the composition.

Picture 2.6

Using this method, you can quickly create a composition with the same dimension of the footage item. However, if you create a composition from a still image, its time duration becomes the previously used time duration. Similarly, you can create compositions from video and audio footage items. By the way, you can also create layers from multiple footage items. In such cases, the layers appear in the layer stacking order in the Timeline panel in the order in which they were selected in the Project panel.

Creating a New Layer

In addition to the standard layers that you create from imported files including compositions, you can also create several other types of layers, such as Text, Solid, Light, Camera, Null Object, Shape Layer, Adjustment Layer, and Adobe Photoshop File. Using the Layer menu or Timeline panel, you can create a new layer. For instance, to create a Text layer, you can either select Layer> New> Text from the Menu bar or right-click an empty space in the Timeline panel and then select New> Text from the context menu.

Now we need to learn about the different types of layers. The following list describes the different types of layers:

Text: Allows you to add text in a separate layer. You can also transform and animate Text layers using the standard layer properties such as position or rotation, as well as unique Text layer properties called text animators.

Solid: Allows you to create a solid layer that can be filled with any solid color. You can use Solid layers as color backgrounds, rectangular shapes, or for effects such as lighting grid effect or beam effect. By default, you can create a solid layer with the composition size. However, you can also create a solid layer with custom size by specifying the width and height values in the Solid Settings dialog box.

Light: Allows you to add light layers (objects) into the composition. However, lights and cameras affect only the 3D layers. Light layers allow you to illuminate 3D layers and cast shadows in a scene to make it realistic.

Camera: Allows you to add a camera layer that simulates the behavior of a real video camera. You can also manipulate the Camera layer to create a sense of movement.

Null Object: Allows you to create an invisible layer that can be used as helper object. You can parent any layer in a composition and control cameras and 3D layers. Null Object layer has all the transformation properties of visible layers such as solid layers.

Shape Layer: Allows you to create a blank vector shape object layer. When you select the Shape Layer option, it activates the shape tool that allows you to create a shape. In addition, when you create shapes using the shape tools, a new Shape Layer is created.

Adjustment Layer: Allows you to create an invisible layer that can be used as the target of effects. You can use Adjustment layers to apply a specific effect or series of effects to multiple layers simultaneously.

Adobe Photoshop File: Allows you to create a new layer and launches the Adobe Photoshop application where you can edit the layer to create visual elements, such as background layer for a composition.

After knowing about the different types of layers, you need to perform the following steps to create a new layer in After Effects:

1. **Open** a project in which you want to create a new layer. Then select **Layer> New> Solid** from the Menu bar. Alternatively, you can press the Ctrl+Y keys together to create a new solid layer. It opens the Solid Settings dialog box.

In our case, the composition size is selected in the Width and Height option. To change the Width or Height option, click the underlined value and type a new value in the text box, and then press the Enter key. Alternatively, when you move the mouse-pointer over an underlined value, a double-headed arrow appears. You can drag it to the left to decrease the value and to the right to increase the value. Click the Make Comp Size button to ensure the current Width and Height options match the composition size.

2. **Click** the color swatch in the Color section and **select** a color in the Solid Color dialog box. In our case, we select the Cyan Solid color. Then click the **OK** button at the end.

When you select a color, the name of the color (Cyan + Solid 1) appears in the Name text box above the Solid Settings dialog box. Solid represents the type of layer and the numeric value represents the number of solid layers in the composition. The new solid layer appears above other layers in the active composition in the Timeline and Composition panels. Similarly, you can create other types of layers, such as Text, Light, Camera, and Null Object.

Understanding Layer Stacking Order

The arrangement of layers in a composition containing multiple layers is called the stacking order. The layer stacking order affects the rendering order and final output. When you add a footage item into a composition, it appears in a new layer and a number is automatically assigned to the layer. By default, these numbers are visible in the Timeline panel before the layer name. When you change the stacking order, the numbers are changed accordingly. For instance, if you move layer 3 to the top of the stacking order, it becomes layer 1 and the rest of the layers are reassigned accordingly.

In the Timeline panel, you can change the layer stacking order by dragging and dropping a layer above or below the target layer. If the layer at the top of the stacking order is fully opaque and the dimension is equal to the composition, the layers below the top layer are invisible. However, if the top layer is transparent or has transparent area, you can see through those transparent areas to the layers beneath. Now perform the following steps to modify the position of a layer in the stacking order:

1. **Click** a layer name in the Timeline panel to select it. In our case, we select the layer named **Stars** which is at the top of the stacking order, as shown in picture 2.7 with the red arrow.

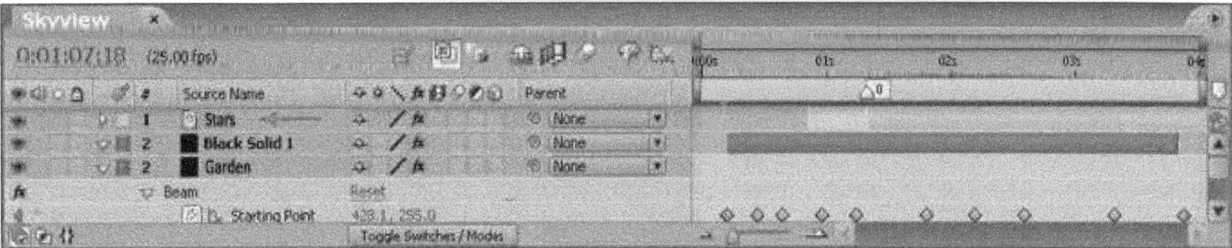

Picture 2.7

2. **Drag** the Stars layer between the layers in the stacking order. In our case, we have dragged the layer between the second and third layer. By the way, when you drag a layer above another layer, a dark solid line appears above the target layer to indicate the position where the dragged layer will be placed in the Timeline panel.

3. **Release** the mouse button to drop the layer. The layer numbering is automatically changed in the stacking order and the Stars layer becomes the second layer in the stacking order and also in the Composition panel.

Exploring Layer Switches

In the Timeline panel, layer switches are arranged in columns. The layer switches are used to define the characteristics of a layer. By default, the A/V Features column appears at the start of the layer switches columns, and the Switches and Modes (Transfer Controls) columns appear to the right of the layer name. You can also show or hide columns by clicking the layer switches, Transfer Controls, or In/Out/Duration/Stretch button at the lower-left corner of the Timeline panel. Pressing the Shift+F4 keys together shows or hides the Parent column. Similarly, pressing the F4 key toggles the display of Switches and Modes columns. You can also arrange these columns in a different order by dragging the name of the column and dropping it over another area. The picture 2.8 shows the layer switches (all the 15 option switches) in a red rectangular box on the left side, and Composition switches on the right side of the picture. The list below the picture 2.8 in the next page briefly describes the layer switches in the Timeline panel:

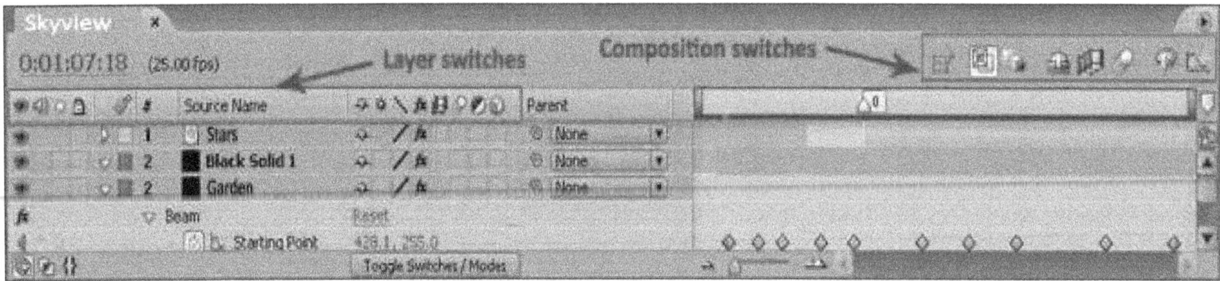

Picture 2.8

Video: In the list of layer switches, this is the first switch (option) from the left side. This switch toggles the visibility of a video of a layer on and off. When the visibility is off, the video can neither be previewed in the Composition panel nor included in the rendering.

Audio: Toggles the audio of a layer on and off. The audio can either be on a separate layer or embedded in a video file.

Solo: Hides those layers without the Solo switch enabled; hence, prevents them from previewing and rendering. When you want to preview only a single layer in a large composition, this switch allows you to isolate those layers with the Solo switch enabled.

Lock: Prevents any kind of modifications of the layer contents. You can enable this switch to prevent accidental changes to the content of a layer. The layer remains visible in the composition and rendering.

Label: Applies a color label to each layer. A default color is applied on a layer based on the type of footage. You can also select a different color from the dropdown list that appears when you click the Label color swatch.

Number: Shows the stacking order of the layers in a composition. The layer numbered 1 always appears at the top of the stacking order. You can select a layer by pressing the corresponding numeric key on the keyboard with a number pad.

Layer/Source Name: Toggles to display a Layer Name and Source Name. The Source Name option displays the name of the footage from the Project panel, while the Layer Name option displays the custom name that you assign to a layer in the Timeline panel. By default, the Source Name option is selected.

Shy: Hides the layer with the Shy mode enabled and the Hide Shy Layers composition switch selected. It removes the Shy layers from the layer display on the Timeline panel, but not from Composition panel.

Collapse Transformations/Continuously Rasterize: Collapses transformation of a layer with a nested composition or pre-composition. It continuously rasterizes a layer that is a shape layer, text layer, or layer with a vector graphic file, such as an Adobe Illustrator file. Generally, the transformations for the nested composition are performed after the masks and effects for the containing composition are rendered. However, when the Collapse Transformations/Continuously Rasterize layer switch is selected, the transformations for the nested composition and the containing composition are combined or collapsed and performed together.

Quality: Specifies how precisely the composition is rendered. You can choose from various modes such as Best, Draft, and Wireframe. The Best mode displays the render at its highest quality; however, takes a long time to render. The Draft mode is a lower-quality preview than the Best mode, and in which certain effects are not rendered. The Wireframe mode displays the outline of a layer and discards all the applied effects.

Effects: Toggles the display of effects on a layer resulting in quicker previews. This switch is disabled until an effect is applied to the layer.

Frame Blend: Removes jerky motion on a video by combining multiple frames together. You can set frame blending to one of three states: Frame Mix, Pixel Motion, or Off. The Enable Frame Blending composition switch must be selected to set the frame blending setting of a layer.
Motion Blur: Toggles motion blur on or off for a layer. You must select the Enable Motion Blur composition switch above the Timeline panel to enable the motion blur setting.
Adjustment Layers: Converts a layer into an adjustment layer when the switch is enabled. When using adjustment layers, the content of the layer is ignored and effects applied to the target layer affect only the layer below it.
3D Layer: Converts a standard 2D layer into a 3D layer. In After Effects, you can apply lights and shadows on 3D layers only.

By the way, pre-compositions are used to group few layers of a composition. This places the layers in a new composition, which replaces the layers in the original composition. Let's now learn to use layer switches to show/hide, lock/unlock, and solo layers in the subsequent sections.

Showing or Hiding Layers

Manipulating layer visibility often plays an important role in a more complex After Effects project. When you add a footage item to the Timeline panel, the visibility of the layer is enabled, by default. You can hide or show a layer at any point of time, while working in a project. Hiding a layer allows you to show and work with the layer below it. In addition, the hidden layer does not appear in the Composition panel as well as in the final output. You can toggle a layer's visibility by clicking the Video layer switch in the Timeline panel. Alternatively, you can also hide or show a layer by selecting Layer> Switches> Video from the Menu bar. Perform the following steps to show or hide a layer in a composition:

1. **Select** a layer that you want to show or hide in the Timeline panel. In our case, we select Wall graphite.JPG layer.
In our case, the layers under the Wall graphite.JPG layer are not visible. So we can hide the layer to show layers beneath it.

2. **Click** the Video layer switch in the Timeline panel for the Wall graphite.JPG layer. This hides the selected layer in the Composition panel and reveals the underneath layer.

You can also hide the hidden layer by selecting Layer> Switches> Video from the Menu bar again or by clicking the Video layer switch in the Timeline panel. You can indentify if a layer is hidden or not by looking at the Video layer switch column in the Timeline panel.

Soloing a Layer

You can separate one or more layers for animating, previewing, or rendering by selecting their corresponding Solo layer switch. This process is known as soloing. When you make a layer solo by selecting the Solo layer switch, all the layers of the same type are excluded from preview in the Composition panel as well as for the final output. For instance, if you select the Solo layer switch for a video layer, all the video layers in the composition are hidden including the still image layers. Soloing does not affect light, camera, and audio layers in a composition; hence, they appear when you preview and render the composition. You can solo one or more layers by selecting the layers in the Timeline panel and clicking the Solo layer switch on the left of the layer name. Here are the steps to solo a layer:

1. **Select** a layer that you want to solo. In our case, we select the TextAnimation.avi layer in the Timeline panel.

2. **Click** the <u>Solo layer switch</u> for the TextAnimation.avi layer. As the result, this video layer switch is dimmed for other layers indicating the other layers are not visible.

When a layer is soloed, its content Is neither previewed in the Composition panel nor included in the final output. In our case, all the layers except the TextAnimation.avi layer are not hidden in the Composition panel.

Locking or Unlocking a Layer

Locking a layer prevents any modification to the layer's content. This helps in preventing accidental changes to the layer that you do not want to modify. By default, a layer is unlocked when you add it in the Timeline panel. Unlike hiding a layer, locked layers remain visible in the Composition panel and are included in the rendering. By default, the Lock layer switch appears in the A/V Feature column. You can click the Lock layer switch of a layer to lock it and re-click the Lock layer switch to unlock it. A lock icon appears in the Lock layer switch for the layer that indicates the layer is locked. Perform the following steps to lock a layer:

1. **Select** a layer that you want to lock in the Timeline panel of your screen. In our case, we select the Stars layer.

2. **Click** the <u>Lock layer switch</u> for the Stars layer to prevent the layer from being edited. Alternatively, press the Ctrl+L keys together to lock a selected layer. As the result, a lock icon appears and the selection highlight is disabled.

The locked layer is also deselected on the Composition panel; however, it remains visible on the Composition panel. The properties for the locked layer, such as position, opacity, and scale, are disabled preventing it from modifications.

Shying a Layer

Managing layers become vital while working with hundreds of layers. In After Effects, there are layer switches and composition switches to help you manage layers in a large project. The Shy feature in After Effects allows you to hide layers from the Timeline panel. However, these layers are still visible and remain editable on the Composition panel. This especially helps while working with large number of layers in the Timeline panel. To hide the layers, enable the Shy layer switch for the respective layers and then select the Hide Shy Layers composition switch. This process is known as shying in After Effects. Perform the following steps to shy layers in After Effects:

1. **Click** the <u>Shy layer switch</u> of a layer to enable the Shy mode in the Timeline panel. In our case, we enable the Shy mode for three still image layers. The Shy layer switch icon changes to another icon when it is enabled.

2. **Click** the <u>Hide Shy Layers</u> composition switch to hide the shy layers. All the layers for which the Shy mode is enabled appear hidden in the Timeline panel.

Lesson 7
Working with Layer Properties
In After Effects, you can modify a layer in different ways, namely: using the Composition panel and using the Timeline panel. Both have their advantages; for instance, while using the Timeline panel, you can precisely set layer properties. Likewise, while using the Composition panel, you can use the transform tools to manipulate layer objects. When you manually modify a layer in the Composition panel, the properties for that layer is automatically updated in the Timeline panel. Similarly, when you modify layer properties in the Timeline panel, the modifications also appear in the Composition panel. By default, every layer has five built-in properties, namely: Anchor Point, Position, Scale, Rotation, and Opacity, which are assembled in the Transform group. You can modify and animate these properties to create motion graphics. When you add masks or effects to a layer or convert a layer to a 3D layer, additional properties are added to the existing ones. To display and modify properties for a layer, you must expand the layer outline. In After Effects, you can only animate properties with a stop watch. The properties of a layer include a stop watch that appears before the property name.

You can animate any layer property either individually or animate two or more properties together. When the stop watch is enabled, any change to the property creates a new keyframe at the playhead's current position. You can either change a property using the transform tools, such as Rotation Tool and Selection Tool on the Composition panel or by editing values in the Timeline panel. Let's briefly discuss the five built-in properties in the Transform group:

Anchor point: Defines the reference or registration point of a layer. It is also referred to as the transformation point. By default, the anchor point is at the center of a layer and all transformations, namely: rotation, movement, and scale occur around this point.
Position: Moves the anchor point but not the actual content of a layer. This property specifies the X, Y, and Z coordinates of a 3D layer. The unit of measurement used by this property is pixels.
Scale: Specifies the relative horizontal and vertical sizes of a layer. The default value for both the horizontal size and the vertical size is set to 100%. Higher percentage values enlarge the size of a layer, while values below 100% reduce the size.
Rotation: Rotates a 2D layer around its central axis, which is also called Z-axis. The Rotation property is displayed as a series of numbers, namely: $0x + 0.0^0$, where the first value is the number of complete rotations to make, and the second number is the ending degree value.
Opacity: Specifies the transparency of a layer. The transparency value can be between 0 and 100 percent, where 0% would be fully transparent, and 100% would be fully opaque.

By the way, special layers such as cameras and lights have slightly different set of properties. For instance, both possess a property Point of Interest, which defines the target onscreen area that the light or camera is pointing at. You can show or hide various properties in the Timeline panel I the following ways:

- To expand or collapse a property group, you can click the triangle on the left of the layer name or property group name.
- To expand or collapse a property group and all of its children, you can click the triangle while pressing the Ctrl key on the keyboard.
- To expand or collapse all the groups for selected layers, you can press the Ctrl+` (accent grave) keys together on the keyboard.

- To reveal an effect property in the Timeline panel, you can double-click the property name in the Effect Controls panel.
- To hide a property or property group, click the name of the property in the Timeline panel while pressing the Alt+Shift keys on the keyboard.
- To show only the selected properties or property groups in the Timeline panel, you can press the S key twice on the keyboard.

You can also copy a layer property and paste it onto another layer. You can only duplicate property groups such as shapes, masks, and effects. You cannot duplicate top-level property groups such as Contents, Masks, Effects, and Transforms. The entire layer is duplicated if you attempt to duplicate a top-level property group.

Setting a Layer Property

Footage items that you import often require modification inside After Effects. For instance, the size of a footage item does not essentially match with the composition size. You can set a property in the Timeline panel or in the Effect Control panel, which reflects on the Composition panel. The Effect Controls panel provides sliders and angle controls for those properties not available in the Timeline panel. If multiple layers are selected and you change a property for one layer, then the property for all the selected layers is changed. Following are the various methods to modify the properties:

- Place the pointer over the underlined value for a property, and drag towards the left to decrease the value or towards the right to increase the value.
- Click the underlined value to make it editable and type a new value, and then press the Enter key on the keyboard.
- Right-click the underlined value and choose the Edit Value option. In the Edit Value dialog box that appears, specify a new value.
- Click the underlined value and press the Up Arrow or Down Arrow key to increase or decrease the property value by 1 unit.
- Hold the shift key while pressing the Up Arrow or Down Arrow key to increase or decrease the value by 10 units.
- Hold the Ctrl key while pressing the Up Arrow or Down Arrow key to increase or decrease the value by 0.1 units.
- Click the Reset option next to the property group name to reset the properties in a property group to their default values.
- Right-click the property name and choose the Reset option from the context menu to reset an individual property. If the property contains keyframes, a keyframe is added at the current time with the default value.

By the way, you can change the units for a property by right-clicking the underlined value and selecting the Edit Value option. You can also enter simple arithmetic expressions for property values and other number entries. For example, you can enter 2*3 instead of 6, 4/2 instead of 2, and 2e2 instead of 200. Now perform the following steps to set a layer property:

1. **Select** the layer for which you want to set a property in the Timeline panel. In our case, we select the Housing.JPG layer. Then, **click** the down triangle (v button) in the Label column for the selected layer while holding the Ctrl key down, (shown in picture 2.9 with the red arrow).

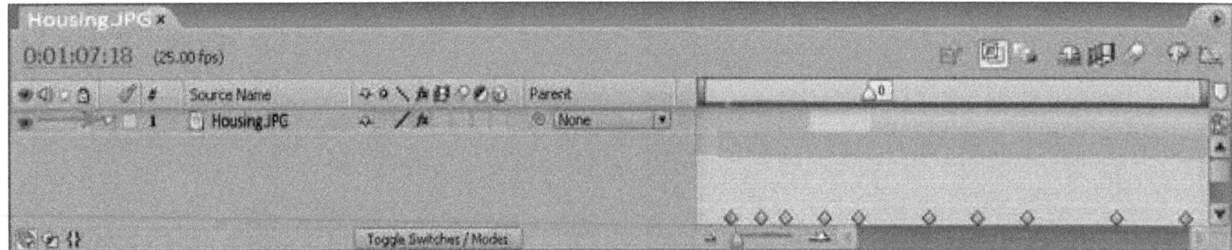

Picture 2.9

This expands the property group and all its sub-properties appear with the default values, as shown in picture 3.0.

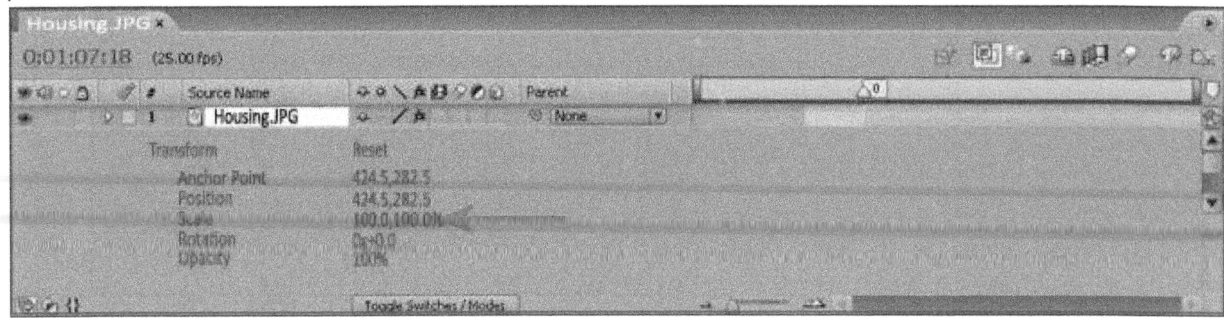

Picture 3.0

2. **Click** and **drag** the underlined value of the Scale property (shown in picture 3.0 with the red arrow). In our case, we increase the Scale property value to 221%.

By default, the Constrain Proportions option is enabled, which allows you to scale in both X and Y axes simultaneously. You can disable this option by clicking the link icon before the underlined values of the Scale property. The Composition panel displays the scaled up Housing.JPG layer.

Applying Blending Modes

As you know, at 100% opacity opaque areas of a layer hide everything below them. To interact between layers in After Effects, you can use blending modes. Blending modes allow you to control the mixing or blending of the content of two or more layers. They also help in producing a multitude of interesting and unusual effects. You can easily apply, change, or discard blending modes with no permanent damage to the layers. The default blending mode for a layer is Normal. If you change a layer's blending mode, it affects only the layers below the active layer, and not he layers above it. You can select a blending mode using the Layer menu or from the Timeline Panel. Perform the following steps to apply a blending mode to a layer:

1. **Open** the composition and **select** a layer in the Timeline panel, for which you want to select a blending mode. In our case, we select Wall graphite.JPG layer.

2. **Click** the Mode dropdown list in the Timeline panel for the Wall graphite.JPG layer, as shown in picture 3.1 with the red arrow. By default, Normal option is selected as the blending mode for Wall graphite.JPG layer.

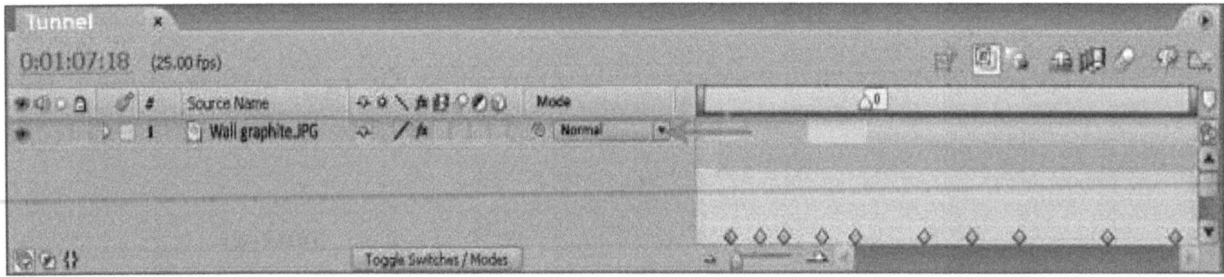

Picture 3.1

3. **Select** a blending mode option from the dropdown list. In our case, we select **Linear Light** option. Alternatively, you can select Layer> Blending Mode> Linear Light from the Menu bar to select a blending mode.

The result of using the Linear Light blending mode is shown in the Composition panel of your screen. Similarly, you can select and apply any of the blending modes as required. Let's briefly discuss about the frequently used blending modes in After Effects CS6:

Normal: Allows each pixel to appear in its original state. The colors of the selected layer do not blend with that of the layer beneath it at 100% opacity. This is the default blending mode.

Dissolve: Works with a layer that has an opacity setting of less than 100%. The effect of Dissolve blending mode appears best on a layer with a lower opacity value. It creates a grainy effect as anti-aliasing is not used. Dissolve blending mode uses random pixels from both the target and the layer below.

Darken: Converts lighter pixels to transparent and retains the darker pixels unchanged. If the pixels on the selected layer are lighter than the layer beneath, the lighter pixels turn transparent. On the other hand, if the pixels on the selected layer are darker, they remain as is.

Multiply: Darkens the colors of the layer by multiplying the color with the layers beneath the selected layer. The final color in the image is always a darker color. This is the most used blending mode.

Color Burn: Searches for the color information in the selected layer and darkens those layers below it in the Layer panel. This blending mode increases the contrast of an image.

Linear Burn: Darkens the layers beneath the selected layer by decreasing the brightness. This blending mode is similar to the Multiply blending mode, but tends to turn specific portions of an image into pure black.

Darken Color: Operates on all channels simultaneously rather than operating on one channel at a time (similar to the Lighter Color blending mode). When blending two colors with this blending mode, only the darker color is visible. This blending mode works similar to the Darken blending mode.

Lighten: Inverse the effect of the Darken blending mode. In this mode, lighter pixels on the target layer remain unchanged; while, darker pixels are replaced with the blend color.

Screen: Searches the channel information of each color, and then multiplies the color applied to the original color resulting in lighter color. It is the opposite of the Multiply blending mode.

Color Dodge: Decreases the contrast to reflect the blend color. It is the opposite of the Color Burn blending mode. If you blend with black, the colors remain unchanged.

Linear Dodge: Reflects the blend color by brightening the base color. It is the opposite of the Linear Burn mode. Using black as blend color produces no change. It is primarily used for tonal and color adjustments.

Lighter Color: Operates on all channels simultaneously. The lighter color is visible when blending two colors with this mode. This blending mode works similar to the Lighten blending mode; however, Lighten blending modes operate only on a single channel at a time.

Overlay: Multiplies the blend colors with the base colors. You can use this mode to preserve the shadows and highlights of an image. It is essentially the combination of two blending modes, namely: Screen and Multiply.

Soft Light: Creates a diffused spotlight effect. You can use this blending mode to correct overexposed photographs or create special effects such as spot focus. The blend colors with 50% or more brightness lightens the image and the blend color with 50% or less brightness darkens the image.

Hard Light: Multiplies the color based on the blend color. The effect is similar to shining a Harsh Spotlight on an image. If the blend color (light source) is lighter than 50% gray, the image is lightened, as though screened. This helps to add highlights to an image. If the blend color is darker than 50% gray, the image appears darker. This helps to add shadows to an image.

Linear Light: Burns or hides the colors by decreasing or increasing the brightness based on the blend color. If the blend color (light source) is lighter than 50% gray, the image is lightened by increasing the brightness. If the blend color is darker than 50% gray, the image is darkened by decreasing the brightness.

Vivid Light: Burns or hides the colors by increasing or decreasing the contrast based on the blend color. If the blend color (light source) is lighter than 50% gray, the image is lightened by decreasing the contrast. If the blend color is darker than 50% gray, the image is darkened by increasing the contrast.

Pin Light: Replaces the colors based on the blend color. If the blend color (light source) is lighter than 50% gray, pixels darker than the blend color are replaced and pixels lighter than the blend color do not change. If the blend color is darker than 50% gray, pixels lighter than the blend color are replaced with colors of layer beneath it in the Layers panel, which leads to darker pixels than the blend color. This is useful for adding special effects to an image.

Hard Mix: Applies a posterization effect based on the selected layer's opacity value. A higher opacity value of the selected layer creates high posterization effect.

Difference: Checks the color information in each channel and subtracts either the blend color from the base color or the base color from the blend color, depending on which has a greater brightness value. Blending with white inverts the base color values, while blending with black color does not produce any change.

Exclusion: Creates an effect similar to, but lower in contrast, than the Difference blending mode. Blending with white inverts the original color. Blending with black produces no change.

Subtract: Looks at the color information in each channel and subtracts the blend color from the base color. In 8 and 16-bit images, any resulting negative values are clipped to zero.

Divide: Looks at the color information in each channel and divides the blend color from the base color.

Hue: Creates the luminance and saturation effect of the base color and the effect of the blend color.

Color: Creates the luminance of the base color and the effect and saturation of the blend color. This preserves the gray levels in the image and is useful for coloring monochrome images.

Luminosity: Creates the effect and saturation of the base color and the luminance of the blend color. This mode creates an opposite effect that of the Color mode.

Applying Layer Styles

In After Effects, layer styles are sets of pre-built effects, such as drop shadow, outer glow, and color overlay. When you import a Photoshop file that includes layers as a composition, you can retain editable layer styles or merge layer styles. You can also choose to ignore the layer styles or merge layer styles into the footage while importing only one layer with layer styles. All the layer styles are preserved in the imported Photoshop file; however, you can only add and modify certain layer styles and controls within After Effects. You can convert merged layer styles into editable layer styles for each After Effects layer based on Photoshop footage at any point of time. You can also apply layer styles in After Effects and animate their properties of them. Following is a list of layer styles that you can apply and edit in After Effects:

Drop Shadow: Adds a soft shadow to a layer. Hence, the layer seems to float in the air creating an illusion of 3D effect. You can specify the color, opacity, blend mode, position, size, and noise values for the layer style.
Inner Shadow: Adds a shadow to the inside boundaries of the layer and creates a recessed appearance.
Outer Glow: Adds a glow that originates outward from the contents of the layer.
Inner Glow: Adds a glow effect to the inside boundaries of the layer.
Bevel and Emboss: Adds a 3D edge effect to the layer. You can specify various settings, such as Style, Depth, Size, Direction, and Angle.
Satin: Applies interior shading that creates a luminous finish.
Color Overlay: Fills the contents of the layer with a solid color. By default, it fills the red color.
Gradient Overlay: Fills the contents of the layer with a gradient.
Stroke: Outlines the contents of the layer.

After learning about the layer styles that you can apply and edit in After Effects, now you can perform the following steps on your computer to apply a layer style on a layer:

1. **Select** a layer in the Timeline panel on which you want to apply a layer style. In our case, we have selected Tunnel.JPG.

2. **Right-click** the selected layer in the Timeline panel and select **Layer Styles> Gradient Overlay** from the context menu.

The Layer Styles property group appears with the Transform group for the selected layer. The Layer Styles property group includes two sub groups: Blending Options and Gradient Overlay. You can see on your screen that the Composition panel displays the default gradient.

3. **Click** the down triangle (v button) before the Gradient Overlay sub-property group in the Timeline panel to expand. This triangle button is to the left of every layer, (already shown in picture 2.9).

4. Select the **Multiply** option from the <u>Blend Mode</u> dropdown list. Then, select the **Diamond** option from the <u>Style</u> dropdown list. After that, set the <u>Scale</u> property to **150%**. As the result, the layer style appears in the Composition panel of your screen.

Similarly, you can also set other properties to modify the Gradient Overlay layer style. For instance, you can edit the gradient colors, smoothness, and opacity. The Opacity option controls the opacity of the layer style. The 0% opacity completely hides the effect of the layer style on a layer. In the same way, you can also apply other layer styles by following the preceding steps; note that the options vary for each layer style. The professional motion picture editors like to use these options while working in After Effects. In the next lesson, we will learn to work with 3D layers.

Lesson 8
Working with 3D Layers

In After Effects, you can work with layers in two dimensions (X, Y) or three dimensions (X, Y, Z). By default, a layer is created in two dimensions. However, you can later convert a 2D layer into a 3D layer. The Z-axis is added to the existing X and Y axes, which represents layer's depth. By combining this depth with a variety of lights and camera angles, you can create animated 3D projects that take advantage of lighting and shadows, perspective, and focusing effects. The 3D layer switch in the Timeline panel allows a layer to be manipulated in three dimensions and also interact with shadows, lights, and cameras. You can convert any layer or composition to a 3D layer except the audio and layer. When you convert a layer into a 3D layer, additional properties, such as Orientation, X Rotation, Y Rotation, and Z Rotation appear in the Transform property group. 3D layers also include the Material Options property group, as shown in picture 3.2.

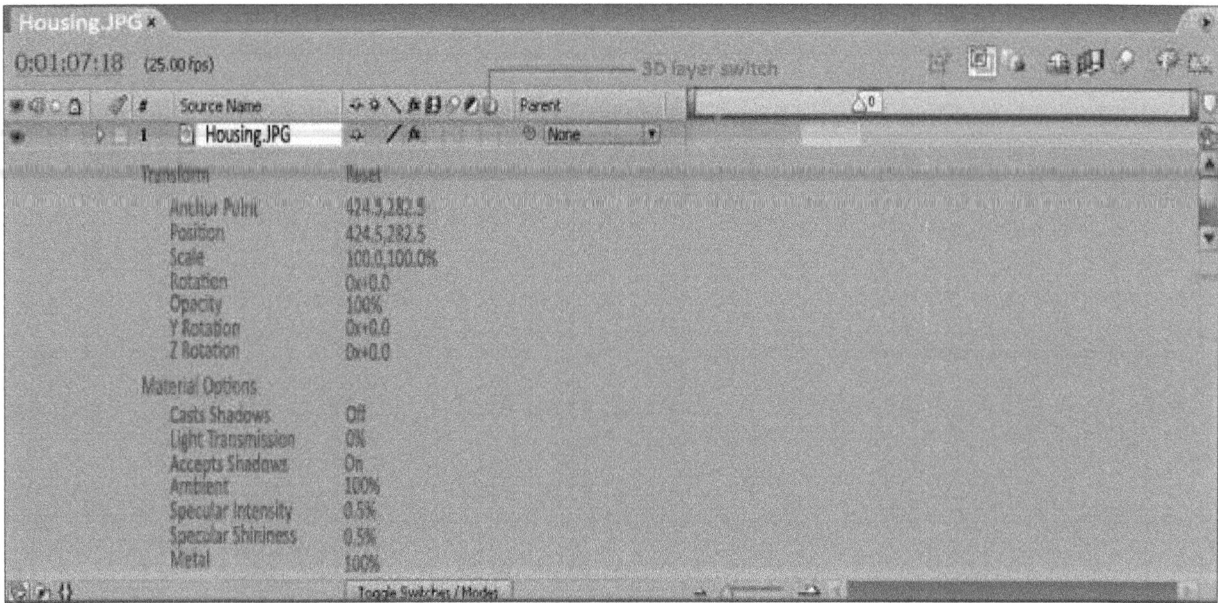

Picture 3.2

The Rotation property is split into X Rotation, Y Rotation, and Z Rotation, and Orientation. The individual rotation properties allow you to create individual keyframes for each axis of rotation. However, animating the Orientation property creates a single keyframe that includes the values of all the three rotation values. Similarly, other properties for the 3D layer, such as Position, Anchor Point, and Scale, include an additional property value for the Z-axis. For instance, the Position option appears in the property list as Position 424.5.0, 282.5, 0.0, where the first value represents its position along the X-axis, the second value represents its position along the Y-axis, and the third value represents its position along the Z-axis.

The Material Options group appears as an additional property group when you enable the 3D layer switch for a layer. Properties in this group specify how the layer interacts with lights and shadows, which determines how realistic the material appears. The Material Options property group includes various properties, such as Casts Shadows, Light Transmission, Accepts Shadows, Accepts Lights, Ambient, Diffuse, Specular, Shininess, and Metal. Now let's discuss the properties available in the Material Options property group:

Casts Shadows: Determines, whether a layer (3D) casts shadows on other layers. The Casts Shadows option is turned off by default. You can choose an option from Off, On, and Only. The Only option makes the layer content invisible but still casts shadows onto the receiving layers. The direction and angle of the shadows are determined by the direction and angle of the light sources.

Light Transmission: Specifies the percentage of light and shines through the layer and casting the colors of the layer on other layers as a shadow. Light Transmission casts a black shadow when no light passes through the layer and the value is set to 0%. The 100% value allows the colors of shadow-producing layer to project onto the receiving layer.

Accepts Shadows: Determines, whether a layer can receive shadows cast by other layers. By default, this option is turned on.

Accepts Light: Determines, whether the color of a layer is affected by light layers in a composition. This setting does not affect shadows. By default, this option is turned on.

Ambient: Specifies the ambient reflectivity of a layer and is non-directional. This setting is most reflective at 100%, and least reflective at 0%. The default value is 100%.

Diffuse: Specifies the diffuse reflectivity of a layer. The diffuse reflectivity is Omni-directional, that is, light is reflected in all directions. This setting is most reflective at 100%, and least reflective at 0%. The default value is 50%.

Specular: Specifies the specular reflectivity of a layer. The specular reflectivity is directional, that is, it reflects back towards the source of the light. This setting is most reflective at 100%, and least at 0%. The default value is 50%.

Shininess: Determines the size of the specular highlight. The default value is 5%. Smaller values produce a larger specular highlight, while higher values produce a smaller highlight.

Metal: Specifies whether the layer's content affects the color of the specular highlight. The default value is 100%. Let's now learn to create a 3D layer in After Effects.

Creating a 3D Layer

As already said, all the layers including compositions are created as 2D layers by default. You can later convert a 2D layer into a 3D layer. You can also combine both 2D and 3D layers together in the same composition. You need to convert a 2D layer into a 3D layer to manipulate the layer in three dimensions. To create a 3D layer, click the 3D Layer layer switch of a 2D layer. Perform these steps to create a 3D layer:

1. **Select** a layer to convert into a 3D layer in the Timeline panel. In our case, we select the TextAnimation.avi layer.

2. Select **Layer> 3D Layer** from the Menu bar to convert the layer into a 3D layer. The 3D Layer layer switch icon appears on the right side of the TextAnimation.avi layer, (shown in picture 3.3 with the red arrow numbered 1). This icon indicates that the layer is a 3D layer.

Alternatively, you can click the 3D Layer switch for the TextAnimation.avi layer in the Timeline panel to convert it into a 3D layer. After converting a layer into a 3D layer, you can modify the layer using various properties specific to 3D layer that appear in both the Transform and Material Options property groups. By default, the Show Layer Controls option is enabled displaying the 3D axes on the selected 3D layer. The 3D axis has three color-coded arrows; red represents the X-axis, green represents the Y-axis, and blue represents the Z-axis. To disable layer controls, you can select View> Show layer Controls from the Menu bar. Let's now learn to transform 3D layer.

Transforming 3D Layers

You can transform a 3D layer similar to a 2D layer using layer's transform properties in the Transform property group. However, the transformation occurs relative to the coordinate space of the composition or the layer. You can also create a custom space by selecting an axis mode. When you convert a 2D layer into a 3D layer, the transform properties, such as Position, Anchor Point, and Scale, include an additional property for the Z-axis. Using these properties, you can manipulate a 3D layer in three dimensional environments. For instance, you can move, rotate, or scale a 3D layer. Perform the following steps to transform a 3D layer:

1. **Select** a 3D layer (TextAnimation.avi layer) in the Timeline panel. Now you can see in the Composition panel (shown in picture 3.3), the 3D axis layer control appears on the 3D layer. To identity the axis, place the cursor over the color-coded arrow to display the axis with the cursor.

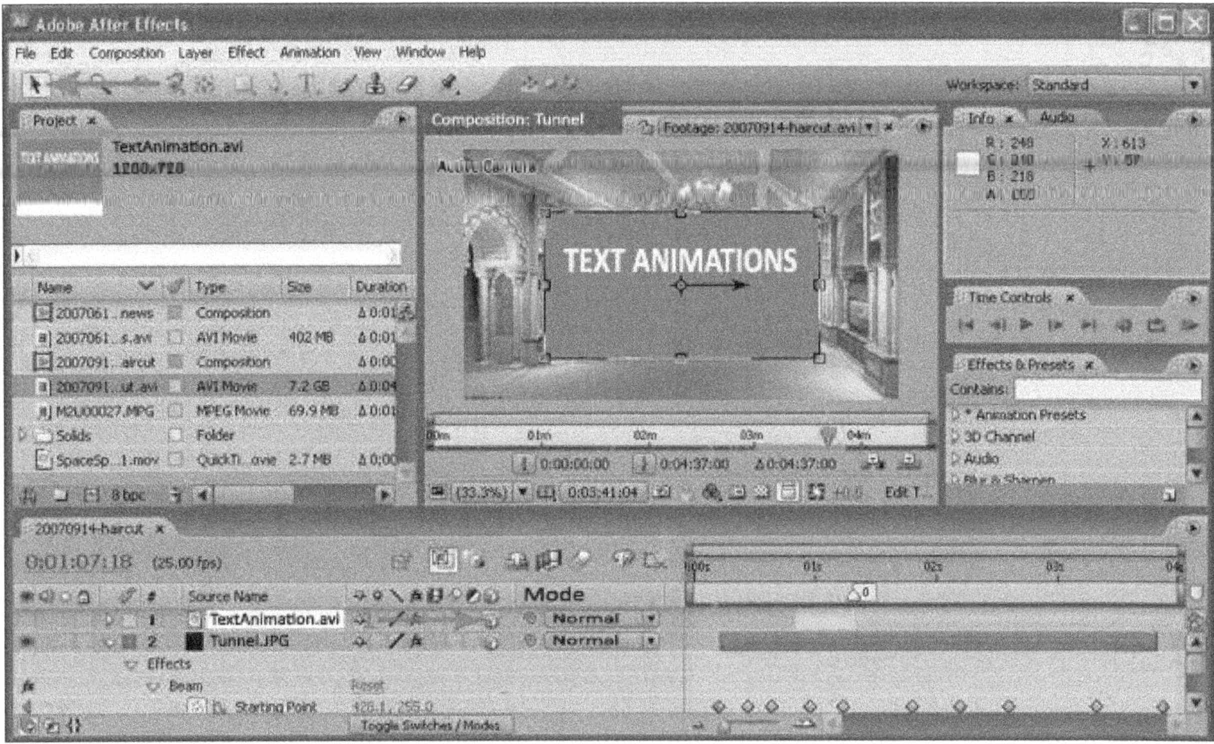

Picture 3.3

2. Select **Selection Tool** from the Tools panel, as shown in picture 3.3 with the red arrow numbered 2 at the top.

3. **Drag** the arrowhead of the 3D axis layer control (on the Composition panel) corresponding to the axis, along which you want to move the layer. In our case, we drag along X-axis.

By the way, while dragging an axis, you can press the Shift key to quickly move the 3D layer. You can also move a 3D layer in the Timeline panel by modifying the Position property values. Now let's proceed and learn to rotate the 3D layer.

4. Select **Rotation Tool** from the Tools panel. Then **move** the cursor over the 3D axis layer control corresponding to the axis along which you want to rotate the layer. In our case, we move over Y-axis.

5. **Drag** the arrowhead of the Y-axis layer control to rotate the 3D layer on the Composition panel, as shown in picture 3.4.

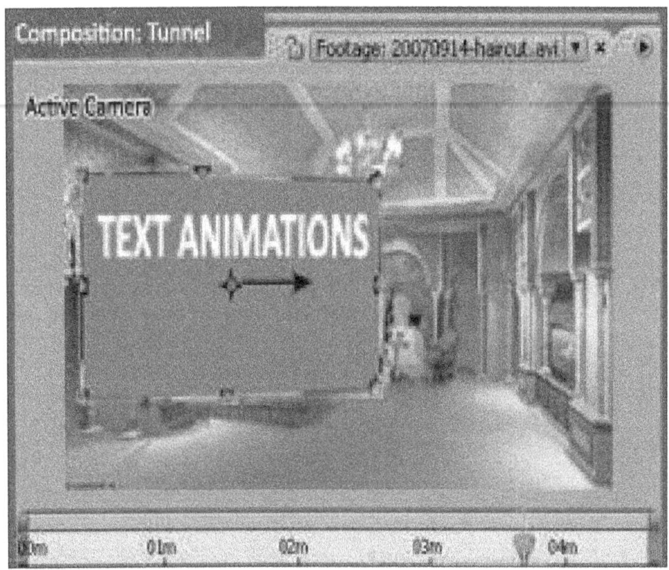

Picture 3.4

If you want to precisely rotate a 3D layer or objet, use the Rotation property for the 3D layer in the Timeline panel. Using the Rotation property, you can type any degree of rotation in their respective axes: X Rotation, Y Rotation, and Z Rotation. In addition, you can use the Orientation property to rotate a 3D layer. The difference between Rotation and Orientation properties can be observed when you animate a 3D layer. The layer rotates directly when you use the Orientation property while it rotates along individual axis when using Rotation property. And, to scale a 3D layer, you can use the Scale property in the Timeline panel. Let's proceed and learn to scale a 3D layer.

6. **Ensure** the 3D layer is selected in the <u>Timeline panel</u> which you want to scale. In our case, the TextAnimation.avi layer is still selected.

7. Press the **S key** on the keyboard to display only the Scale property in the Timeline panel. Then **set** the **Scale** percentage values to: **75%** for each axis. When you set the value for one axis, the other two values simultaneously change as the Constrain Proportions option is enabled, by default. As the result, the 3D layer scales up in the Composition panel.

To quickly select a property, press the corresponding key assigned to the property. Following list describes the keys assigned to each property in the Transform group: Anchor Point = A, Position = P, Rotation and Orientation = R, Scale = S, Opacity = T

Working with Lights

In real life, lights give depth and perspective to a scene and make it more engaging and realistic. They can be used to illuminate 3D layers and cast shadows. You can also use lights to relate to a lighting situation in a scene into which you are compositing or to create more interesting visuals. In After Effects, a light is a type of layer that you can add to shine light on other layers. Lights do not affect 2D layers; however, you can convert a 2D layer into a 3D layer. For instance, you can use light layers to create the appearance of light streaming through a video layer. You can also animate settings for a light to create the animated light effects; however, you cannot animate the light type and the Casts Shadows property. When you create a new light, you can change the settings for the light; but depending on the type of light, certain settings are disabled. For instance, when Point is selected as the light type, the Cone Angle and Cone Feather settings are disabled. The Light Settings dialog box appears when you create a light by selecting Layer> New> Light from the Menu bar. You can also double-click a light layer in the Timeline panel to open the Light Settings dialog box. In addition to the Light Settings dialog box, you can modify the light settings in the Light Options property group in the Timeline panel.

Adding a Light

Lights in After Effects allow you to add sense of realism to a composition. Select Layer> New> Light from the Menu bar to create a light. You can add multiple lights in a composition in After Effects. When you create a light, a new light layer is always created at the top of the layer stacking order in the Timeline panel. By default, lights always focus to a point of interest, which appears at the center of the composition. Using the Point of Interest property in the Transform property group, you can modify the point of interest. You can also modify the lights, using various settings, such as Intensity, Color, and Cone Angle. The effect of lights is only visible on the opaque parts of 3D layers. Perform the following steps to add a light in After Effects:

1. **Create** a new composition or open an existing composition. In our case, we open an existing composition (Tunnel) with multiple 3D layers.

2. **Select** a layer in the Timeline panel on which you want to add a light. In our case, we select TextAnimation.avi layer. In case you try to add a light on a 2D layer, the Warning message box appears confirming that camera and lights do not affect 2D layers.

3. Choose **Layer> New> Light** from the Menu bar to create a new light. It opens the Light Settings dialog box on the screen.

4. **Type** a name in the Name text box as: **Text Animation**. Then **click** the color swatch for the Color option and **select**: Lime color in the Light Color dialog box.

5. Select the **Casts Shadows** check box to enable the light to cast shadows. Then click the **OK** button in the Light Settings dialog box. As the result, the light layer is created at the top of the stacking order in the Timeline panel and the light appears on the Composition panel.

On your After Effects screen, you can see the effect of light on the layers in the Composition panel. The light brightens the layers making the edges much darker. This is caused by the Cone Angle and Cone Feather settings when the Light Type is set to Spot.

Modifying Light Settings

As already learned, a new light is created with the default settings that appear in the Light Settings dialog box. Later, you can modify these settings in the Light Options property group of the Timeline panel, as required. You can also double-click a light layer in the Timeline panel to open the Light Settings dialog box for the selected light layer. The light layer includes the Light Options property group along with the commonly used Transform property group. You can click the triangle to the left of the Light Options property group to display various properties. Perform the following steps to modify the properties for a light:

1. **Click** the down triangle (v button) to the left of Text Animation layer in the Timeline panel, (already shown in picture 2.9).

2. **Click** the down triangle to the left of the Light Options property group to display various properties with their default settings. Then **set** the Intensity option to **200%**, and set the Cone Angle option to **150%**. The modified light effect appears on the Composition panel.

Similarly, you can set the light settings as required. You can also cast shadow on an object using the Casts Shadows property in the Light Options property group. The Casts Shadows property adds shadows to a layer; however, you must have a layer with transparency to be able to see the shadow. The opaque area casts shadow on the background layer. For instance, you can add shadow to a text layer. In this case, both the text layer and the background layer must be a 3D layer and the Casts Shadows option must be selected in the Material Options property group for the background layer. Let's understand the common light properties, which are given as follows:

Light Type: Lets you specify the type of light that you want to create. You can create the following four different types of light in After Effects:
- Parallel: Emits directional unrestricted lights; for instance, lights cast by the Sun.
- Spot: Emits lights in a conical direction and is restricted to the cone shape. Spot lights are directional lights that project a cone of light at the subject. By default, a Spot light is selected for the Light Type option.
- Point: Emits unrestricted Omni-directional light, similar to a light bulb in real world.
- Ambient: Adds light to the overall brightness of a 3D scene. The Ambient light lacks a source and does not cast shadows.

Intensity: Defines the strength of the light, which is calculated in percentage. Values above 100 percent produce a burned-out effect on those layers where the light falls; while negative values reduces the brightness of the layer. By default, the Intensity value is set to 100%.

Color: Specifies the color of the light source. The default color is set to White.

Cone Angle: Specifies the angle of the cone that constrains the source light and affects the diameter of the light. By default, the Cone Angle value is set to 90%. This setting is enabled only for the spotlight.

Cone Feather: Specifies the softness of the cone's edge. By default, the Cone Feather value is set to 50%. This setting is enabled only for the spotlight.

Casts Shadows: Specifies, if the light causes layers in a 3D scene to cast shadows onto it. The shadows need to have a surface to be cast on.

Shadow Darkness: Specifies the darkness of the shadow. This setting is enabled when the Casts Shadows option is selected.

Shadow Diffusion: Specifies the shadow's softness. The amount of softness is based on the value set and the shadow's distance from the layer casting it. This setting is enabled when the Casts Shadows option is selected.

Working with Cameras

In After Effects, cameras are designed to simulate the real world camera. Cameras are 3D objects that you can manipulate in a 3D environment similar to lights in After Effects. You can view 3D layers from any angle and distance using camera layers. You can also pan, tilt, and move the camera to create engaging compositions. In addition to the transform properties of the camera layer, you can animate the Camera Options properties that are unique to cameras in After Effects. You can use properties, such as Zoom, Focus Distance, and Blur Level, to simulate those effects as in real-world cameras, such as Depth of Field and Rack Focus. Cameras affect only 3D layers; however, they can also affect 2D layers with the Comp Camera attribute. You can use the active composition camera or lights to view or light an effect from various angles to simulate refined 3D effects with effects that have a Comp Camera attribute. After Effects CS6 includes the easy-to-use 3D camera tracker feature, which is useful to effectively integrate 3D objects into a 2D scene.

Unlike still images and video layers, light and camera layers do not include the Anchor Point property; instead, they have a property called Point of Interest. This property appears in the Transform property group in the Timeline panel. The camera focuses at the point of interest. When you move a camera, it always rotates to focus at this point. All the cameras are listed in the 3D View menu at the bottom of the Composition panel from where you can select a camera any time. You can select to view a composition through the active camera or through a custom camera. The active camera is the topmost camera in the Timeline panel at the current time for which the Video switch is selected. The active camera view is the point-of-view used for creating the final output and nesting compositions. If you have not created a custom camera, then the active camera is the same as the default composition view.

Let's learn about the camera properties in After Effects. The professional motion picture editors use these properties quite often white editing a movie. Following are the various camera properties that you can use to manipulate a camera:

Zoom: Specifies the distance from the camera lens to the subjects in the 3D scene.
Depth of Field: Toggles the depth of field for a camera. If the Depth of Field property is enabled, it simulates a camera that focuses at one depth (focal plane) in a 3D scene, and blurs objects at other depths.
Focus Distance: Specifies the distance from the camera lens at which a layer is in focus.
Aperture: Specifies the size of the opening in a camera lens, and this option also affects the camera's depth of field.
Blur Level: Specifies the amount of blur produced by a camera's Depth of Field effect.

Adding and Manipulating a Camera

To add cameras into a composition, you need to select Layer> New> Camera from the Menu bar. Alternatively, you can also right-click an empty area on the Timeline panel, and then select New> Camera from the context menu to create a camera. In the Camera Settings dialog box, you can specify various camera settings. After creating the camera, you can use the Camera Options property group in the Timeline panel to specify the camera settings. By default, the new camera layers begin at the start of the composition duration. However, you can choose to begin the new layers at the current time indicated by the playhead by deselecting the Create Layers at Composition Start Time option in the Preference dialog box. Perform the following steps on your computer to add a camera to a composition in After Effects:

1. **Select** the composition into which you want to add a camera. In our case, we select the Tunnel composition.

2. **Right-click** an empty area in the Timeline panel, and then select **New> Camera** from the context menu. The Camera Settings dialog box appears, as shown in picture 3.5.

3. **Type** the name in the Name text box: **Camera for Tunnel**, as shown in picture 3.5 indicating with the red arrow. Then, for Preset option, select **80 mm** camera preset.

4. **Select** the Enable Depth of Field check box to enable the depth of filed. Then click the **OK** button to create a camera with the specified settings.

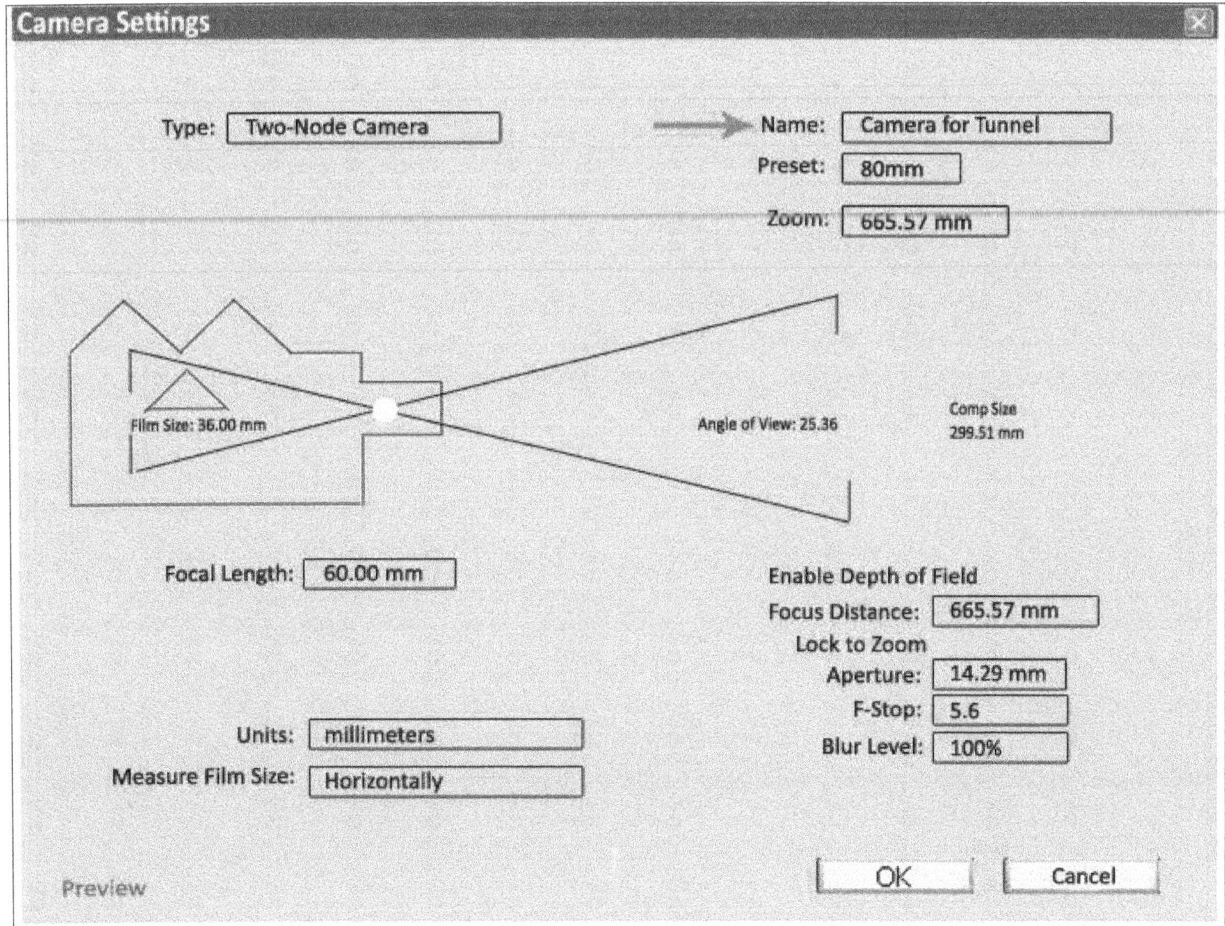

Picture 3.5

The Camera for the Tunnel camera layer appears selected at the top of the stacking order in the Timeline panel.

5. Select the **2 Views – Horizontal** option from the Select view layout dropdown list at the bottom of the Composition panel. As the result, the Composition panel displays two views. By default, the 1 View option is selected in the Select view layout dropdown list. You can display maximum of 4 views on the Composition panel.

Now you can see on your screen, the 2 Views – Horizontal option displays the Top view to the left and the Active Camera view to the right of the Composition panel. You can click inside a camera view to make it active. The options at the bottom of the Composition panel serve for the active view when multiple views options are selected in the Select view layout option.

6. **Select** the camera layer in the Timeline panel. Then select **Hand Tool** from the Tools panel or press the H key to select it.

7. **Click** and **drag** the Hand Tool cursor in the Top view (on Composition panel) to pan the view until you can see the rectangular camera icon. Depending on the screen size and monitor resolution, you may need to change the magnification amount for this view. You can scroll down to zoom out.

8. Select **Selection Tool** from the Tools panel. Then **place** the Selection Tool cursor above the rectangular camera icon in the Top view (on Composition panel) and drag to change the camera view. You can see the change in the active camera view in the Composition panel.

9. **Move** the camera icon closer to its point-of-interest to zoom in. If you want to zoom out, you can move the camera icon away from the point-of-interest.

The camera has a gizmo when selected. If you position Selection Tool over one of the arrows in the gizmo, it allows you to constrain the movement of the layer to that specific axis. Moving the camera changes the relationship of the layers on the screen. The background does not cover the entire composition space when viewed from camera's new position. In the next section, let's learn about 3D camera tracker in After Effects CS6.

Tracking 3D Camera Movement

After Effects CS6 includes the easy-to-use 3D camera tracker feature, which is useful to effectively integrate 3D objects into a 2D scene. It allows you to extract camera motion as well as 3D scene data by analyzing the video clip. To analyze footage and extract camera motion, you need to select Animation> Track Camera or Effect> Perspective> 3D Camera Tracker from the Menu bar. The extraction process is processed in the background. After the process is over, small colored x's appear on the footage, which are called tracking points. Tracking points help to place the 3D objects into a scene. The size of the points signifies those points that are closer to the camera. Perform the following steps to track 3D camera movement in After Effect CS6:

1. **Create** a composition and **import** the video in which you want to track 3D movement. In our case, we create a composition named Rain and import the Rain 02.mp4 video footage item.

2. **Add** the Rain 02.mp4 footage item onto the Rain composition by **dragging** the footage item over the Timeline panel, (already shown in picture 2.6).

3. Select **Effect> Perspective> 3D Camera Tracker** from the Menu bar to apply the 3D camera tracker. As the result, After Effects analyzes the video clip indicated the by the message on the Composition panel of the footage.

You can see on your screen that the Effect Controls panel appears when you select the 3D Camera Tracker option. After a few seconds, the 3D track points (small crosses) appear known as tracking markers. When you move the mouse pointer over the tracking markers, a target symbol appears showing the current plane. To ensure that the correct plane is selected, you can select multiple tracker points. To select multiple tracking markers, click and drag over them. You can drag the target symbol around the plane to see if the perspective matches.

After mapping the track points, you may want to refine them. Before refining, you can check the Average Error value under the Advanced tab of the Effect Controls panel. The Average Error setting defines the average distance between the 3D solve points and the 2D track points. It represents the scene mapping accuracy. Ideally, any value below 1.0 indicates higher mapping accuracy. To refine, you have to just remove the unnecessary tracking points. With this, we come to the end of this lesson of creating and using the 3D camera tracker in After Effects CS6.

Lesson 9
Drawing and Painting

Drawing refers to the process of creating geometric shapes called vector objects. In After Effects, you can either create parametric shapes using built-in shape tools or create custom shapes using Pen Tool. Typically, a shape consists of a path, stroke, and fill. To modify a shape, you need to modify its path, which is the outline of the shape. A path consists of straight or curved line segments and vertices. The area enclosed inside a path is called the fill of a shape; the thickness of the path or outline is called as the stroke of a shape. You can use solid, semi-transparent, or gradient colors as the fill and stroke of a shape. Using the Fill Options and Stroke Options dialog box, you can configure the fill and stroke options. When you create a shape, a shape layer is created in After Effects. You can modify a shape using its properties in the Timeline panel. In addition, you can use path operations, such as Repeater and Pucker & Bloat to alter parametric or pen-based shape paths to create new shapes. Painting refers to changing the colors of pixels in a layer. Using After Effects paint tools such as Brush Tool, Clone Stamp Tool, and Eraser Tool, you can paint brush strokes called vector objects. In After Effects, you cannot paint on the Composition panel; instead, you can use the Layer panel to paint. Each brush stroke has its own properties, which you can modify in the Timeline panel. In After Effects, a brush stroke is named after the tool with which you create it. For instance, if you create a brush stroke using Clone Stamp Tool, it is named as Clone 1. The numeric value specifies the number of brush stroke created using the tool. In this lesson, you first learn about shape tools and their options. You also learn to create parametric shapes and modify them. Next, you learn to draw custom shape using Pen Tool, edit a shape, and apply path operations, such as Repeater and Pucker & Bloat.

Working with Shape Tools

Using Shape tools you can create parametric vector shapes, such as rectangle, ellipse, and star. You can also create abstract backgrounds. In After Effects, there are various shape tools, such as Rectangle Tool, Rounded Rectangle Tool, Ellipse Tool, Polygon Tool, and Star Tool. You can access a shape tool from the Tools panel. When you start After Effects, Rectangle Tool is selected by default. You can also press the Q key on the keyboard to cycle through the five shape tools. In addition to the five shape tools, Pen Tool is available, which helps to create custom shapes. You can also copy a shape from masks as well as other programs, such as Photoshop or Illustrator. In After Effects CS6, a new tool called Mask Feather Tool has been introduced, which controls the feather around a mask. You can access Mask Feather Tool from the Pen Tool flyout. To cycle between Pen Tool and Mask Feather Tool, press the G key on the keyboard. You will learn more about Mask Feather Tool in the following lessons.

Shape tools also allow you to create masks in After Effects. Similar to shapes, masks are vector objects used to hide or reveal a portion of a layer. You can create masks by drawing with the shape tools or Pen Tool on the Composition panel. You can create masks depending on the type of selected layer in the Timeline panel. There are certain rules in After Effects, which determines whether you want to create a shape layer or mask. The rules are as follows:

- If no layer is selected in the Timeline panel, a shape is created.
- If a non-shape layer is selected in the Timeline panel, a mask is created.
- If a shape layer is selected in the Timeline panel, the **Tool Creates Shape** and **Tool Creates Mask** buttons on the Tools panel determine whether the shape tools or Pen Tool create a shape or mask. By default, the Tool Creates Shape button is enabled, which allows you to create shapes. To create masks, enable the Tool Creates Mask button on the Tools panel.

Without any layer selected in the Timeline panel, you select a shape tool or Pen Tool, additional options for fill and stroke of the shape appear on the <u>Tools panel</u>. The options include Fill Options, Fill Color, Stroke Options, Stroke Color, Stroke Width, and Add Attribute. The Tool panel is already shown in picture 1.2. By the way, to deselect all the layers in the Timeline panel or Composition panel, you need to press the F2 key on the keyboard.

Exploring Built-In Shape Tools
As already learned, to draw parametric shapes, After Effects provides five built-in shape tools. You can access these tools from the Tools panel. By default, Rectangle Tool is selected and other tools are hidden below it. A small triangle in the lower-right corner of the default shape tool indicates that one or more additional tools are hidden behind it. To access other tools, press and hold Rectangle Tool. A flyout appears with the list of all shape tools, such as Rectangle Tool, Rounded Rectangle Tool, Ellipse Tool, Polygon Tool, and Star Tool. A brief description of the available shape tools is as follow:

Rectangle Tool: Allows you to create parametric rectangular shapes or masks by dragging on the Composition or Layer panel. By default, Rectangle Tool is active when you launch After Effects. You can also use this tool to square shapes. To create a square shape, you need to hold the Shift key down while dragging the tool.
Rounded Rectangle Tool: Allows creating rounded rectangle shapes, or masks by dragging on the Composition or Layer panel. You can also create rounded square shapes using this tool. To create a rounded square, hold the Shift key down while dragging the tool. While drawing a rounded rectangle, you can increase or decrease the corner roundness. Press the Up Arrow or Down Arrow key without releasing the mouse button to increase or decrease the corner roundness of the shape, respectively.
Ellipse Tool: Allows you to create elliptical shapes or masks by dragging on the Composition or Layer panel. You can also create circular shapes by holding the Shift key down while drawing a shape. To draw the shape from the center, drag the cursor while holding the Shift key, and then press the Ctrl key. To create a mask, select a layer before drawing.
Polygon Tool: Allows you to create polygonal shapes. In After Effects, a polygon is a star shape without the Inner Radius or Inner Roundness property. Hence, a shape created for a polygon in the Contents group is called Polystar. To add or remove sides to a polygonal shape, press the Up Arrow or Down Arrow key, or scroll the mouse wheel forward or backward while creating it. By default, Polygon Tool creates a polygon with five sides.
Star Tool: Allows you to create star shapes or masks by dragging on the Composition or Layer panel. While creating the shape, you can simultaneously rotate it. To prevent the shape from rotating, hold the Shift key down. Similar to Polygon Tool, the name of the shape created for a star in the Contents group is Polystar. You can add or remove points by pressing the Up Arrow or Down Arrow key, or scrolling the mouse wheel forward or backward. You can also increase or decrease the outer roundness by pressing the Left Arrow or Right Arrow key.
Pen Tool: Allows you to draw custom shapes or masks with Bezier paths. After creating a shape or mask, you can refine it using Add Vertex Tool, Delete Vertex, and Convert Vertex Tool. With a layer selected, you can create a Bezier mask using Pen Tool. You can create a shape on a new shape layer when no layer is selected.

Each shape tool retains the most recent settings. For instance, if you draw a polygon with eight sides, any other polygon that you draw later will also have eight sides. You can reset the options to its default by double-clicking a tool on the Tools panel.

After Effects adds a new shape layer to a composition when you draw a shape directly on the Composition panel. Each shape layer includes various shape attributes that appear in the Timeline panel. By default, the shape layer is named as Shape Layer 1 in the Timeline panel, where the numeric value (1) represents the number of shape layers in the composition. In addition, the shape name appears in the Contents group; for instance, if you create a rectangle, the name appears as Rectangle1. You can also apply stroke and fill settings to shape, modify its path, and apply animation presets.

Exploring Shape Tool Options

When you select a shape tool or Pen Tool, additional options appear on the Tools panel including Fill Options, Fill Color, Stroke Options, Stroke Color, and Stroke Width. You can modify these options before or after creating a shape. These options remain the same for shapes that you create consecutively unless you modify them. Certain options are disabled when you select a particular type of layer. The picture 3.6 shows the various options that appear when a shape tool or Pen Tool is selected:

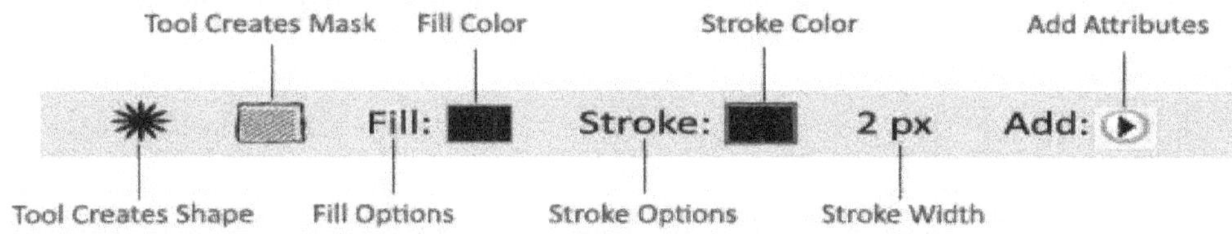

Picture 3.6

Tool Creates Shape: Enables you to create shapes instead of masks with no layers selected. If a shape layer is selected, this setting enables you to add a new shape to the existing shape layer.

Tool Creates Mask: Enables you to create masks instead of shapes if a non-shape layer is selected in the Timeline panel. If a shape or any other layer is selected, it creates a mask.

Fill Options: Allows you to select a solid color or a gradient for a shape based on whether the fill is enabled or disabled or the fill is a solid color or gradient. You can modify these properties in the Fill Options dialog box. To open the Fill Options dialog box, click the underlined word Fill on the Tools panel. In the Fill Options dialog box, you can also set the blending mode and transparency for the fill. The default blending mode is Normal, the default fill type option is Solid Color and the Opacity value is set to 100%. You can also fill a shape with linear or radial gradients.

Fill Color: Allows you to select a color for a shape. By default, Solid Color is selected as the fill type. You can click the Fill Color swatch button next to Fill Options to open the Shape Fill Color dialog box to select a color. If you set fill type as gradient, the Gradient Editor dialog box appears on clicking the swatch button. To cycle through the fill type options, click the Fill Color swatch button while holding the Alt key down.

Stroke Options: Allows you to set options to enable or disable a stroke or to make the stroke a solid color or gradient. You can open the Stroke Options dialog box by clicking the underlined word Stroke on the Tools panel. In the Stroke Options dialog box, you can also set the blending mode and transparency for a stroke. By default, Normal is selected as the blending mode. The default stroke type is selected as Solid Color and the Opacity value is set to 100%. You can also apply linear or radial gradients to strokes.

Stroke Color: Allows you to select a color for a stroke. By default, the stroke color is set to Solid Color. You can also select gradient as the stroke color. You can click the Stroke Color swatch button to open a Shape Stroke Color dialog box to select a stroke color. If you set the stroke type to gradient, the Gradient Editor dialog box appears when you click the Stroke Color swatch button.

Stroke Width: Allows you to set the appearance of strokes; by default, it is set to 2 px. Pixel is the default unit of measurement for the stroke width. You can set the value by dragging the underlined Stroke Width numeric value. You can also click the numeric value and type any other value.

Add: Allows you to add attributes to a shape layer. It is enabled only when a shape layer is selected in the Timeline panel. You can click the arrow button next to the Add option to display the list of attributes.

You can also access the options in the Add menu from the Timeline panel. By default, the new attributes are inserted into the selected shape group or groups. For instance, the new paths are added below the existing paths and groups.

Drawing a Parametric Shape

As already learned, you can create a parametric shape by drawing with a shape tool or Pen Tool. You can also modify the attributes of a parametric shape. For instance, you can modify the width and height of a rectangle shape after creating it. By default, if you draw on the Composition panel with a shape layer selected, you can create a new shape within that shape layer above the previously created shapes or group of shapes. However, if you draw with an image layer other than a shape selected, you can create a mask.

You can then add shape attributes to the existing shapes or create new shapes within that shape layer. You can also convert a text layer to shapes on a shape layer using the Create Shapes from Text command from the Layer menu. There is an advantage of using a shape layer instead of a solid layer, you can use the Fill Options dialog box to create a linear or radial gradient. For instance, you can create a gradient background for the composition by creating a rectangle of the composition size and fill the rectangle with either the linear or radial gradient. In After Effects, you can create shapes and shape layers using any of the following methods:

- Create a new, empty shape layer by selecting Layer> New> Shape Layer from the Menu bar.
- Draw a path using a shape tool or Pen Tool.
- Convert a text layer to a shape layer by selecting Layer> Create Shapes from Text from the Menu bar with the text layer selected. You can also convert a mask path to a shape path.
- Paste a path copied from another layer or from Adobe Illustrator, Photoshop, or Fireworks.

You have learnt about creating shapes in After Effects. To do it practically, you can perform the following steps to draw a parametric shape:

1. **Select** the composition in which you want to draw the shape. In our case, we select the Hot Air composition in the Shapes.aep project.

It shows the name 'Hot Air' at the top left of the Timeline panel, and 'Shapes.aep' at the top left in the Title bar of the After Effects screen, as shown in picture 3.7 with red arrows numbered 1 and 2.

2. **Press** the F2 function key to deselect all the selected layers in the Timeline panel. Then **select** a shape tool (Rectangle Tool) in the Tool panel.

3. **Click** and **drag** the cursor on the Composition panel to draw a rectangle, as shown in picture 3.7 with the red arrow numbered 3. To move a shape while creating, you can hold the Spacebar key down.

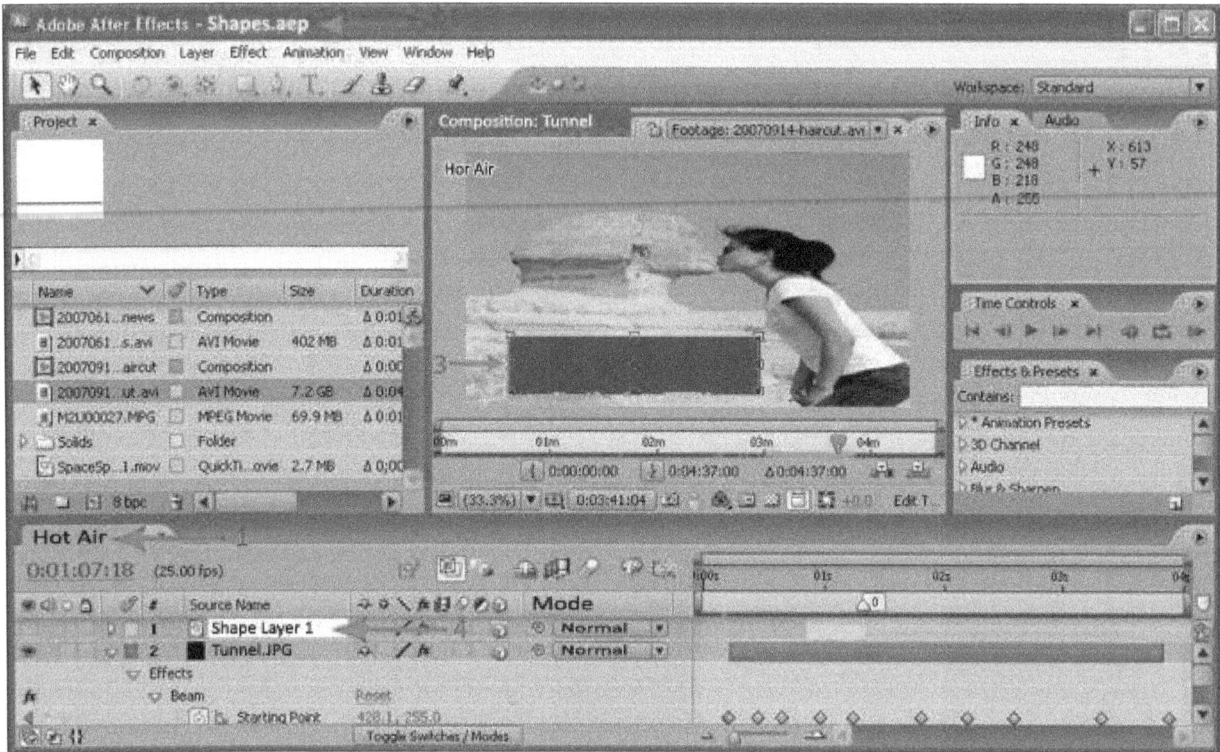

Picture 3.7

As you can in the picture as well as on your screen, the rectangular shape has fill and a stroke that corresponds to the settings on the Tools panel. After Effects also adds a shape layer at the top of the layer stacking order, called Shape Layer 1 in the Timeline panel, as shown in picture 3.7 with the red arrow numbered 4. Similarly, you can draw other shapes like rounded rectangles, ellipses, polygons, and stars by selecting the respective tools from the Tools panel and drawing on the Composition panel.

Modifying a Shape

After you create a shape, you can modify it as required. For instance, you can modify the properties for the shape layer in the Timeline panel or use the bounding box to modify the shape on the Composition panel. In the Timeline panel, a basic shape group typically consists of a shape path, the Stroke and Fill operators, and a set of Transform properties. The Contents property group is the master group that contains various shape added to the layer. Perform these steps to modify a shape using Timeline panel:

1. **Create** the shape on the Composition panel using a shape tool. In our case, we create a **star** shape using the Star tool.

2. In the Timeline panel, **expand** the layer of the star you created by clicking the down triangle button. Then **expand** the **Polystar 1** group and then expand the **Polystar Path 1** subgroup in the Timeline panel.

3. Set the **Points** property to: 15.0, **Inner Radius** to: 140.0, and **Outer Radius** to: 300.0. You can also combine various properties to create interesting shapes. For instance, you can modify the values of the Inner Roundness and Outer Roundness properties to create pinched shapes.

4. Set the **Inner Roundness** to: 81.0%, and **Outer Roundness** to: -220.0%. As the result, the modified star shape appears on the Composition panel of your screen.

Using Pen Tool to Create Shapes

Pen Tool is the most advanced shape tool in After Effects. It offers wide variety of editing capabilities and helps you to create freedom shapes and paths, such as complex curved shapes. A path is an outline that represents a series of smooth straight (vector) lines. Paths are independent of resolution and can be scaled up to any size. Using Pen Tool, you can create straight paths as well as smooth flowing curved paths. You can also create either a shape or a mask using this tool. The simplest path that you can draw using Pen Tool is a straight line. Click with Pen Tool to create straight line segments connected by corner points. In addition, you can use Add Vertex Tool and Delete Vertex Tool to add and remove vertices. You can also modify a path using Convert Vertex Tool. To access these tools, hold Pen Tool down to display a flayout with the tools. You will see on your screen that the RotoBezier check box appears on the Tools panel when Pen Tool is selected. Those paths created with the RotoBezier option enabled, do not have Bezier handles. Smooth path between vertices is automatically calculated. You can also convert any manual Bezier path to a RotoBezier path without changing the curvature of the path. Perform the following steps to create a shape using the Pen Tool:

1. **Create** a composition and **import** a JPG image. Then **add** the image item onto the composition by **dragging** the item over the Timeline panel. You will see that the JPG image layer is selected in the Timeline panel. Now to create a shape, you need to deselect any non-shape layers.

2. **Press** the F2 function key to deselect any selected layer. Then **select** the Pen Tool from the Tools panel or press the G key to activate Pen Tool.

3. **Set** any preferred Pen Tool options, such as color, fill type, and stroke width on the Tools panel. In our case, we use the default settings.

4. **Move** the cursor on the Composition panel to start the path and **place** the first vertex (point). Then **click** to place the first vertex. The first vertex appears as a solid square indicating that it is selected. By the way, the unselected vertices are displayed as a hollow square.

5. **Move** the cursor elsewhere and **click** to place the second vertex. Similarly, **add** multiple vertices in the background image. Then **move** the cursor over the first vertex and **click** to close the path when a closed circle icon appears.

If you want, you can reposition a vertex after you have placed it before releasing the mouse button, by holding the Spacebar key down on the keyboard, while dragging the mouse. You will see on your screen that the shape is filled with red and the stroke is filled with white color. If you want, you can create curved segments by clicking and dragging the direction line handle. You can also close a path by double-clicking the last inserted vertex. However, this method creates a straight line segment by joining the first and last vertices. If required, you can also leave the path open by selecting another tool, or by pressing the F2 key to deselect the path.

To create a C-shaped curve, drag the direction line away from the previous direction line, and then release the mouse button. Similarly, you can create an S-shaped curve by dragging the direction line in the same direction as the previous one.

Lesson 10
Editing a Shape

In After Effects, mostly you need to tweak a shape after creating it on the Composition panel. To edit a shape, you need to modify its underlying path. While modifying a path, you need to add more vertices or move the unnecessary vertices as required. You can edit the shape using various tools, such as Add Vertex Tool, Delete Vertex Tool, and Convert Vertex Tool. To add or remove vertices, use Add Vertex Tool and Delete Vertex Tool, respectively. Adding vertices to the path allows you to make intricate curves, corners, and blends.

A path consists of one or more straight or curved segments. On curved segments, each selected vertex display one or two direction lines ending in direction points. You can also reposition vertices to make smooth paths. Using Convert Vertex Tool, you can change the direction of a selected point's curve on an existing path. The positions of the direction lines and points determine the size and curvature of the path. You can click an existing vertex to reset the curve, or click and drag the vertices to change the curve. Ensure the Toggle Mask and Shape Path Visibility button is enabled on the Composition panel. You can also select individual vertex and move them to modify a shape. Perform the following steps to edit a shape in After Effects CS6:

1. **Expand** the shape layer containing the shape that you want to modify in the Timeline panel. In our case, we expand Shape Layer 1 created in the previous lesson. By the way, to expand a parent layer as well as its children, click the arrow to the left of the parent layer while holding the Ctrl key down.

2. **Select** the Path 1 property under the Shape 1 property group to select the path and display the vertices in the Composition panel.

3. **Press** the V key on the keyboard to activate Selection Tool. Then **select** a vertex that you want to modify, by clicking it. When you select a vertex, it appears with a solid square.

4. **Drag** the selected vertex to any other location. In our case, we move the selected vertex to a different location.

You can also modify the path by dragging the direction handles with Selection Tool selected. Using Pen Tool, you can also add or remove vertices. In most cases, the appropriate Pen Tool becomes active when you place the Pen Tool cursor in a particular context. For instance, Add Vertex Tool becomes active when you place the Pen Tool cursor over a path segment. You can also use Convert Vertex Tool to modify a vertex. This tool toggles a vertex between a smooth point and a corner point.

5. **Select** Pen Tool from the Tools panel or press the G key. Then **move** the Pen Tool cursor over the path except vertices; a plus sign (+) appears attached to the Pen Tool cursor. Alternatively, you can select Add Vertex Tool from the Tools panel to add vertices.

6. **Click** the path where you want to add a new vertex. In our case, we click on the straight path segment. A new vertex appears on the straight path, and is selected by default.

7. **Select** Convert Vertex Tool from the Tools panel and **move** the Convert Vertex Tool cursor over a vertex. Then **click** and **drag** to convert the corner point to a smooth point. If needed, you can hold the Alt key down to activate Convert Vertex Tool when Pen Tool is selected.

Using Path Operations

Path operations are used to modify a shape's path nondestructively. They are similar to effects, which are also nondestructive in After Effects and apply to all paths in the same group. You can add attributes such as path operations to a shape layer after creating it using the Add option on the Tools panel or in the Timeline panel. You can rearrange path operations by dragging, cutting, copying, and pasting them on the Timeline panel. You can apply shape operations, such as Fills and Strokes, on the modified path. If you include several shape paths or groups inside a different group and apply a shape effect to it, all the shape paths and groups are affected as a single group. You can also animate the changes using keyframes. Following are the path operations in After Effects:

Merge Paths: Combines paths into a single compound path. This operation considers all the paths above the selected path in the same group as input and combines them. The input paths remain visible in the Timeline panel, but they are essentially removed from the rendering of the shape layer. Fill and Stroke properties are appended the Merge Paths property group in the Timeline panel if not available already.

Offset Paths: Expands or contracts a shape by offsetting a path from the original path. A positive Amount value expands the shape, while a negative Amount value contracts it.

Pucker & Bloat: Pulls the vertices of a path inward or outward, while curving the line segments. It takes the line segments between the vertices of a shape path and either curves them inward (pucker) or bends them outward (bloat).

Repeater: Creates multiple copies of a shape and applies a specified transformation to each copy.

Round Corners: Creates smooth path by rounding the corners. A higher Radius value increases the roundness.

Trim Paths: Animates the Start, End, and Offset properties to trim a path. When applied to an open path shape, or fill is set to none, this effect can also be used to draw a stroke on and off. When you create a new shape, the strokes as well as effects such as Trim Paths originate from the top-most vertex, which is the first vertex. To change the first vertex for a path created with Pen Tool, right-click on any vertex and select Mask and Shape Path> Set First Vertex from the context menu.

Twist: Rotates a path more sharply in the center than at the edges. A positive value twists the shape path clockwise, while a negative value twists it counterclockwise.

Wiggle Paths: Wiggles a path by converting it into a series of jagged peaks and valleys of various sizes. The distortion is animated automatically; it changes over time without the need to set any keyframes or add expressions.

Wiggle Transforms: Wiggles any combination of the position, vertex, scale, and rotation transformations for a path.

Zig Zag: Adds jagged or rounded ripples to the shape path.

Using the Repeater Path Operation

Repeater allows you to create multiple copies of a shape. This is most advanced path operation, which takes underlying shape and repeats it several times, as required. You can use the Offset property to place the copies in the Composition panel. The Offset property value is used to offset the transformations by a specific number of copies. The Repeater path operation creates virtual copies of all paths, strokes, and fills above the path in the same group. The virtual copies are not represented by separate entries in the Timeline panel; instead, they are rendered in the Composition panel. Each copy is transformed based on its order in the set of copies and the values of the properties in the Transform property group for that instance of the Repeater. Here are the steps to create multiple copies of a shape using the Repeater path operation:

1. **Select** any shape layer containing a shape. In our case, we select Shape Layer 1 containing the same shape we had created in the previous lesson.

2. Click the **Add** property in the <u>Contents property</u> group, (already shown in picture 3.6). A drop-down list appears with the built-in path operations.

3. Select the **Repeater** option from the dropdown list. The Repeater path operation is applied to the selected layer. By default, three copies of the shape is created and distributed on the Composition panel. You can modify the various attributes for the Repeater path operation using the Repeater 1 property group in the Timeline panel.

4. **Expand** the Repeater 1 property group to display the properties. You can also press the U key twice to expand all the properties simultaneously. To contract the property groups, press the U key once. To maximize the Timeline panel, press the ` (tilde) key on the keyboard.

5. Set the **Copies** property to 18.0 in the Repeater 1 property group. Then set the **Offset** property to 2.0 in the Repeater 1 property group. And then, set the **Position** property to 115.0,40.0 in the Transform: Repeater 1 property group.

6. Set the **Scale** property to 89.0, 89.0% in the Transform: Repeater 1 property group. Then set the **Rotation** property to 0x + 51.0^0 in the Transform: Repeater 1 property group. And then, set the **End Opacity** property to 35.0% in the Transform: Repeater 1 property group.

The result of all the changes appears on the Composition panel. Suppose, you are modifying parametric shapes such as polygons and stars; by default, the Repeater property group appears below the Fill and Stroke property by groups in the Timeline panel. In this case, each copy of the shapes is filled and stroked individually. However, if you place the Repeater 1 property group after the Path property (Polystar Path 1) and above the Fill and Stroke property groups for the shape, the copies are filled or stroked as a compound path. Similarly, you can experiment with other options in the Repeater 1 property group to create complex shapes and effects.

Using the Pucker and Bloat Operation

Pucker & Bloat is one of the several powerful path operations included in After Effects. The operation involves pulling the vertices of a path inward or outward, all the while curving the line segments. This allows you to create several interesting shapes. When you apply Pucker & Bloat path operation on a path, each line segment either curves inward (called pucker) or outward (called bloat). You can further modify its properties in the Timeline panel. To pucker a shape, set the Amount property to a negative value. To bloat a shape, set the Amount property to a positive value. Perform the following steps to use the Pucker & Bloat operation:

1. **Select** a shape layer containing any shape to apply the Pucker & Bloat path operation. In our case, we select the Shape Layer 1 containing a **star shape**.

2. Click the **Add** property in the <u>Contents property</u> group. Then select the **Pucker & Bloat** option from the dropdown list. You will see that the Pucker & Bloat path operation is applied on the selected shape layer.

The Pucker & Bloat 1 group adds to the Contents property group in the Timeline panel and the default settings apply to the shape on the Composition panel. You can further modify the properties for the Pucker & Bloat path operation in the Pucker & Bloat 1 group in the Timeline panel.

3. **Expand** the Pucker & Bloat 1 property group in the Timeline panel to display the properties. The Pucker & Bloat path operation contains only the Amount property, which is by default 10.0. As discussed, negative values pucker a shape and positive values bloat it.

4. Set **Amount** property to any value. In our case, we set it to **-40.0**. As the result, the star shape reflects the change as per Amount value on the Composition panel. The negative value puckers the star shape.

Working with Paint Tools

In After Effects, there are several paint tools to apply brush strokes on a layer and modify the color or transparency of an area in the layer. You can apply brush strokes on the Layer panel. However, it does not modify the source layer. Brush strokes are vector objects that can be scaled up without losing quality. There are three paint tools in After Effects, namely: Brush Tool, Clone Stamp Tool, and Eraser Tool. Brush Tool, as the name suggests, works similar to a real world paintbrushes. It paints smooth strokes with the foreground color selected in the Paint panel. Whereas, Clone Stamp Tool allows you to replicate pixels from the layer and paint them to create clones; Erase Tool removes pixels and creates transparent areas. The mouse-pointer appears as a circle icon when you select a paint tool indicating the current position of the tool.

By default, Brush Tool produces soft-edged strokes or lines. Although jagged edges are most apparent in diagonal lines, anti-aliasing is applied to brush stroke edges. You can specify settings for a brush stroke before applying it using the Paint and Brushes panels. By default, there are several sample brush presets, such as Hard Round 19 pixels and Soft Round 21 pixels, in the Brushes panel. You can work with these presets and modify them to create new brushes. Using the Brushes panel, you can specify brush settings, such as Diameter, Roundness, and Angle. Using the Paint panel, you can specify brush settings, such as Set Foreground color, Set Background color, Opacity, Flow, and Mode. Let's now discuss the common paint tool settings available in the Paint panel:

Opacity: Determines the maximum amount of paint applied on a layer, while using Brush Tool or Clone Stamp Tool, and the maximum amount of paint and layer color removed, while using Eraser Tool.
Flow: Determines the speed at which paint is applied, while using Brush Tool or Clone Stamp Tool, and the speed at which the paint and layer colors are removed, while using Eraser Tool.
Mode: Determines how pixels in the underlying image are blended with the pixels painted on by Brush Tool or Clone Stamp Tool strokes.
Channels: Determines the channels of the layer Brush Tool stroke or Clone Stamp Tool is affected by stroke. The stroke only affects opacity while using the alpha channel. Painting an alpha channel layer with black removes pixels and creates more transparent areas. You can create same using Eraser Tool.
Duration: Determines the duration of a brush stroke. You can select different options for the Duration setting, such as Constant, Single Frame, Custom, and Write On. The Constant option applies the stroke from the current frame to the end of the layer duration. The Single Frame option applies the stroke only to the current frame. The Custom option applies the stroke to the specified number of frames from the current frame. The Write On option applies the stroke from the current frame to the end of the layer duration and animates the End property of the stroke to match the motion.

Using Brush Tool

Using Paint tools, you can create brush strokes with the current foreground color. By default, the foreground color is set to red. To create a brush stroke, drag the cursor on the Layer panel with Brush Tool selected. By default, if you release the mouse button while painting brush strokes, the stroke is stopped; if you drag the cursor again, a new stroke is created. All the new strokes appear as separate entry in the Timeline panel. However, you can drag the cursor while holding the Shift key down to continue drawing the previous stroke. By default, each brush stroke is named after the tool that created it, with a number which indicates the order in which it is created. You can also modify various settings for a paint tool before drawing the brush strokes. You can later modify and animate these brush strokes to create interesting animation effects. Each brush stroke has its own duration bar, Stroke Options properties, and Transform properties that you can modify in the Timeline panel. Perform the following steps to paint brush strokes using Brush Tool:

1. **Double-click** a layer in the Timeline panel on which you want to paint brush strokes. Then select **Brush Tool** from the Tools panel. When you select a paint tool, the Brushes and Paint panels appear in the workspace.

2. Set the **Diameter** value to **45 px** in the Brushes panel to set the brush size. To set the color for Brush Tool, click the Set Foreground color swatch in the Paint panel. In our case, the default values are used for all other settings.

3. **Click** and **drag** on the Layer panel with the Brush Tool cursor to paint. The Layer panel is already shown in picture 2.5. You can draw a brush stroke by holding the Shift key down.

You can see on your screen that the Effects property group is added when you draw a brush stroke. If you create multiple brush strokes, all strokes are listed as separate entity, namely: Brush 1, Brush 2, Brush 3, and so on. The Brush 1 group lets you transform the brush stroke using properties, such as Stroke Options and the Transform: Brush 1. The Blend Mode dropdown list allows you to set a blending mode for the brush stroke. By default, the Blend Mode selected is Normal.

4. **Select** a blending mode for the brush stroke from the Blend Mode dropdown list. In our case, we select Multiply. The brush stroke blends with the background image layer and appears as part of the background.

Using Clone Stamp Tool

You must be familiar with Clone Stamp Tool if you have used Adobe Photoshop. Clone Stamp Tool in After Effects works similar to Photoshop. It is used for retouching and repainting portions of a layer as well as clone or duplicate selected areas of a layer. Similar to Brush Tool, you can use Clone Stamp Tool only on the Layer panel. To use Clone Stamp Tool, you need to set a sampling point on the area you want to copy (or clone) the pixels from and paint over another area. Clone Stamp Tool paints one part of layer, the sampled pixels over another part of the same layer or another layer. To sample pixels, hold the Alt key down and click the pixels on the Layer panel.

You can use different brush tips for Clone Stamp Tool to precisely control the size of the clone area. Using the Opacity and Flow settings that appear on the Paint panel, you can control the painting of the cloned area while using Clone Stamp Tool along with other settings, such as Source and Mode. In addition, you can select the Aligned check box to shift the sample point (Clone Position) for subsequent strokes to match the movement of Clone Stamp Tool in the target Layer panel. In simple words, with the Aligned check box selected, you can use multiple strokes to paint on one copy of the sampled pixels. In contrast, if the option is disabled, the same sample point is retained between strokes; you start painting on pixels from the original sample point every time you drag the mouse-pointer to create a new clone stroke. Perform the following steps to clone an area using Clone Stamp Tool:

1. **Create** or select a composition that contains <u>both</u> the source and target layers. In our case, we select Hot Air composition.

2. **Double-click** the source layer in the Timeline panel to open it in the Layer panel. Then **select** Clone Stamp Tool from the Tools panel.

3. **Set** the brush tip using the <u>Diameter</u> option in the <u>Brushes panel</u>. The Brushes panel appears on the right side of After Effects screen. In our case, we set it to: 76 px.

4. **Move** the Clone Stamp Tool cursor over any area of the source layer to pick the sample. Then **click** any area on the source layer to use as sample pixels while holding the <u>Alt key</u> down. A crosshair identifies the point being sampled to help you identify what Clone Stamp Tool is sampling as you apply clone strokes.

5. **Select** the target layer using the Layer panel tab dropdown list. The Layer panel is already shown in picture 2.5. Then **move** the cursor over any area and **paint** the sampled pixels.

Using Eraser Tool

Eraser Tool allows you to remove pixels from a layer that creates transparent areas. The pixels of the layer below appear to be merged with the selected layer. You can select various modes for Eraser Tool in the Paint panel. The Layer Source & Paint or Paint Only mode creates eraser strokes that you can modify and animate in After Effects. In contrast, using the Eraser tool in the Last Stroke Only mode only affects the last brush stroke drawn and does not create an Eraser stroke. The Layer Source & Paint is the default mode for Eraser Tool. Perform the following steps to use Eraser Tool on a layer:

1. **Open** a layer on the Layer panel by double-clicking it in the <u>Timeline panel</u>. Then select **Eraser Tool** from the Tool panel.

The Auto-Open Panels checkbox on the Tools panel allows you to display the Brushes and Paint panels automatically when you select a paint tool. You can also use the Toggle the Paint panel button to toggle the panels display.

2. **Select** the brush tip from the list of <u>presets</u> in the <u>Brushes panel</u>. Then **paint** over any area on the Layer panel to erase. If you drag the cursor with Eraser Tool selected, it paints the area black in the Composition panel

3. **Click** the Composition tab to activate the Composition panel that shows the transparent area. The result will be shown in the Composition panel.

Lesson 11
Working with Animation

Animation involves creating motion using stationary objects. Theoretically, animation is an illusion of movement. It occurs when a sequence of still images or frames are transmitted over a period of time. In After Effects, animating objects or layers is very important for creating motion graphics. To animate a layer, you must animate its Transform properties available in the Timeline panel. It includes properties such as Position, Rotation, Scale, and Opacity. For instance, using Position property, you can animate a layer from position A at time zero to position B at time 10 seconds mark to move the layer. Any property with a stop watch button on its left in the Timeline or Effect Controls panel can be animated.

In After Effects, there are keyframe-based animations for which you can use keyframes for creating animations. A keyframe is the point in time to specify a value for a layer property. Values for all other frames between two keyframes (in-between) are automatically calculated in a keyframe-based animation. For smooth animations, use frames that slightly vary from each other. In addition, you can create complex animations using animation presets. In this lesson, you first learn to work with keyframes. Next, you learn to animate a layer transformation. Further, you learn to edit a motion path to modify an animation. You will also learn to animate a 3D layer, null object, and animate a camera.

Working with Keyframes

In keyframe animation technique, specifying keyframes is the most important and the trickiest part. A keyframe holds a value that represents a major change in the movement of an object. After Effects interpolates the unspecified values for the frames between keyframes. This process is known as interpolation or tweening. Interpolation between keyframes can be used to animate movements, effects, audio levels, image adjustments, transparency, and color changes. When the stop watch is active for a specific property, a keyframe is created for the property at the current time on changing the property value. If you change the value for a layer property while the stop watch is inactive, that value remains the same for the duration of the layer. Picture 3.8 shows active and inactive stop watches as well as keyframes in the Timeline panel.

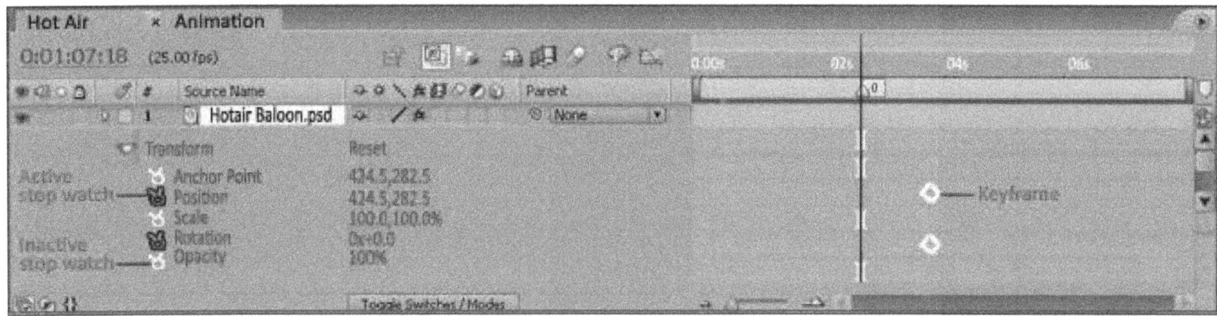

Picture 3.8

If you deactivate the stop watch, all keyframes for that layer property are deleted, and the constant value for the property becomes the value at the current time.

Adding Keyframes Manually

When the stop watch is active for a specific property and you modify the property, a keyframe is automatically added at the Current Time Indicator (CTI). If there is an existing keyframe at the CTI, its values are modified. To add keyframes for a layer property manually, click the corresponding stop watch icon appearing on the left of the layer name in the Timeline panel. The new keyframe is selected when you add it and appears as a diamond shape. When the stop watch for a layer property is inactive (the default case), and you modify the property, it does not affect an existing keyframe or adds a new keyframe at the CTI. Perform the following steps on your computer to add a keyframe for a layer property:

1. **Create** a composition and **import** the footage items that you want to use. In our case, we create the Animation composition and import the Hotair Balloon.psd footage item. The picture 3.9 shows the composition's name "Animation" with the red arrow numbered 1.

2. **Select** a layer for which you want to add a keyframe and **expand** its Transform property group in the Timeline panel. In our case, we select the Hotair Balloon.psd layer.

3. **Select** a property from the <u>Transform</u> property group. In our case, we select **Position** property, as shown in picture 3.9 with the red arrow numbered 2.

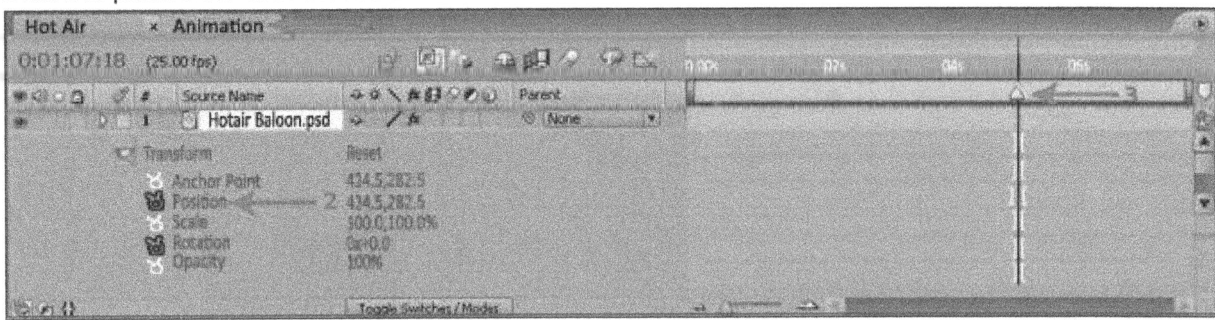

Picture 3.9

4. **Move** the CTI to any frame to add a keyframe. In our case, we move the CTI to the frame at 5 seconds mark, as shown in picture 3.9 with the red arrow numbered 3. If you want to precisely move the CTI to 5 seconds mark, click the <u>Current Time</u> button on the top left of the Timeline panel, type 500 in the text box, and press the Enter key.

5. Click the **Time-Vary stop watch** icon button (shown in picture 3.8 as Active stop watch) on the left of the Position property name in the Timeline panel. As the result, a new keyframe is added at the CTI based on the Position property in the timeline.

After adding a keyframe, you can modify its Position property value. The keyframe stores the value until you modify it again. Similarly, you can add multiple keyframes for any property at different frames by moving the CTI to that frame. You can add a keyframe for each property at a single frame. To add a keyframe, move the CTI to a particular frame and click the stop watch for the property.

Adding Keyframes Automatically

The Auto-keyframe mode in After Effects allows you to add keyframe automatically. When the Auto-keyframe mode is on, modifying a property automatically enables the Time-Vary stop watch button for that property and adds a keyframe at the current time. By default, this mode is turned off; to activate it, select the Auto-keyframe properties when modified composition switch is enabled in the Timeline panel. Perform the following steps to add keyframes automatically:

1. **Expand** the layer properties in the Timeline panel. In our case, we expand the properties of the Hotair Balloon.psd layer.

2. **Move** the CTI to any frame in the timeline. In our case, we move it to 5 seconds mark. Then click the **Auto-keyframe properties when modified** composition switch in the Timeline panel. This switch is shown in picture 4.0 with the red arrow. When you click, it makes the layer switch enabled.

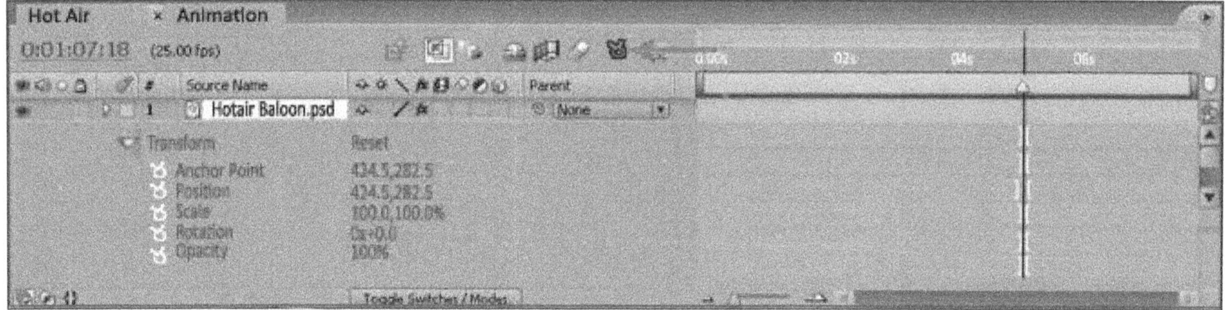

Picture 4.0

3. **Change** the value for any property that you want to modify. In our case, we set the Scale property to 70.0, 70.0%. As soon as you change the property, After Effects automatically adds a keyframe at the CTI which you can see on your screen.

You can also see on your screen that the Time-Vary stop watch is enabled automatically. Similarly, you can add multiple keyframes at different CTI positions and properties. As long as the Auto-keyframe mode is turned on, After Effects adds keyframes when you modify a property value.

Editing a Keyframe

When the Time-Vary stop watch button for a layer property is enabled, you can change the property value to add a new keyframe. A new keyframe is automatically added at the current frame, or if any value for the selected frame exists, it is updated. It also allows you to change the value of an existing keyframe any time. To change a keyframe value, select the keyframe and enter the value in the respective field. This helps you to change the values whenever required. In addition, you can right-click a selected keyframe and select the Edit Value option from the context menu. You can also edit the values of multiple keyframes simultaneously. Select multiple keyframes by holding the Shift key down and click the keyframes. By the way, while modifying the value for a keyframe, you need not move the CTI to the keyframe. To select a keyframe, either click it or drag a marquee around it. The selected keyframes appear as yellow diamonds. Now perform the following steps to edit a keyframe:

1. **Select** a keyframe in the timeline for which you want to edit the value. In our case, we select the Scale property keyframe.

2. **Right-click** the selected keyframe, and select the **Edit Value** option from the context menu. It opens the Scale dialog box. Alternatively, you can also double-click the keyframe to open the Scale dialog box.

3. **Click** the underlined value for the Width option and **enter** a value. In our case, we enter 100. As you can see in the Scale dialog box on your screen, the Constrain Proportions option is enabled by default; hence, the Height value automatically changes to 100% on changing the Width value.

4. Click the **OK** button in the Scale dialog box to change the keyframe value. If you want, you can also change the value in the Timeline panel. Instead of using the Scale dialog box, you can use the underlined values for a property in the Timeline panel to modify the value.

Copying and Pasting Keyframes

In After Effects, you can copy the keyframes from one layer (the source layer) and paste them onto another layer (the target layer). You can use this feature to copy an animation in a layer onto other layers. When you paste keyframes onto another layer, they appear in the corresponding property of the destination layer. The first keyframe appears at the current frame indicated by CTI of the destination layer, and the other keyframes follow in relative order. You can also move the keyframes to the destination layer timeline by drag and drop method.

However, you cannot copy keyframes from multiple layers simultaneously. You can copy keyframes between layers for the same property, such as Position, or between different properties that use similar data, such as the values of the Position and Anchor Point properties. You can also copy and paste the same properties between two layers simultaneously. For instance, you can copy multiple properties, such as Position, Scale, and Anchor Point, simultaneously from a layer and paste them onto the similar properties of another layer. However, while copying and pasting between different properties, you cannot copy multiple properties. You can only copy one property and paste it to a different property at a time. Perform the following steps to copy and paste keyframes from one layer to another layer:

1. **Select** an animated layer (Hotair Balloon.psd). Then **select** the property containing the keyframes that you want to copy. In our case, we select the Rotation property.

By the way, you can press the R key on the keyboard to expand only the Rotation property. In our case, the Rotation property contains three keyframes, which are highlighted. If you want to select multiple keyframes, drag over them in the timeline or click multiple keyframes while holding the Shift key down.

2. Select **Edit> Copy** from the Menu bar. Then **select** a destination layer in the Timeline panel onto which you want to paste the keyframes. In our case, we select the Sky.jpg layer.

3. **Move** the CTI to a point where you want the keyframes to appear. In our case, we move it to 5 seconds mark in the timeline.

4. Select **Edit> Paste** from the Menu bar or press the Ctrl+V keys together to paste the keyframes on the selected layer. The keyframes appear for the Rotation property of the Sky.jpg layer.

5. **Press** the R key to display the Rotation property for the Sky.jpg layer. You will see that the first keyframe appears at 5 seconds, while the second and third keyframes appear relative to first keyframe.

6. **Preview** the animation. You can see that the animation for both the layers is the same with a time difference of 5 seconds. To preview an animation, press the **Spacebar** key; however, it does not preview in real-time. You can preview an animation in real-time using the **Preview panel**.

To paste keyframes to a different property, select a destination property. By default, the keyframes are pasted on the same property it is copied from. The next lesson is about animating layer transformation.

Lesson 12
Animating Layer Transformations

Layer transformation refers to the modification of layer properties. In After Effects, you can modify the properties and animate the transformations as well. For instance, you can move, scale, or rotate a layer from one position to another, and animate this movement over a period of time using keyframes. In After Effects, there are five built-in properties, namely: Anchor Point, Position, Opacity, Rotation, and Scale that you can modify to transform a layer. In addition, you can also animate these properties. For instance, you can animate layer rotation using the Rotation property in the Timeline panel. The Rotation property also allows you to rotate a layer around its anchor point. The first part of the Rotation property value is the number of whole rotations, while the second part is the fractional rotation in degrees. You can animate properties in the Transform property group with a stop watch. The process of animation is similar for all properties. You can animate the changes over time by placing keyframes for each change. Perform the following steps to animate the transformation of a layer:

Picture 4.1

1. **Select** a layer in the Timeline panel that you want to animate and **expand** its properties. In our case, we select the Hotair Balloon.psd layer.

The picture 4.1 shows the Balloon image (image 1) selected on the background image (image 2) in the Composition panel.

2. **Click** the Time-Vary stop watch button for the property that you want to animate. In our case, we click the Position property button. As you can see on your screen, a new keyframe is added at the first frame in the timeline.

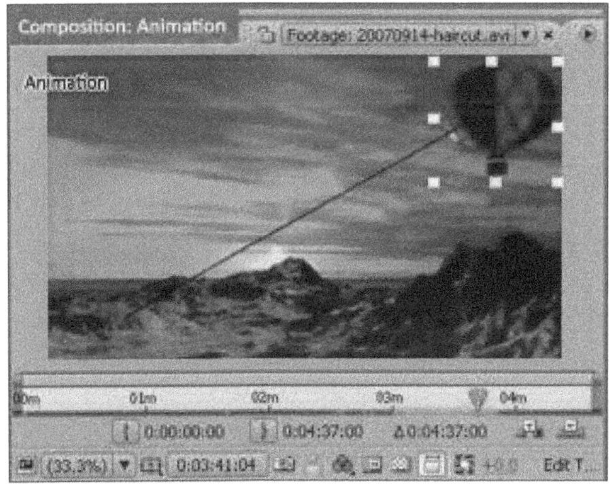

Picture 4.2

3. **Drag** the CTI to another frame (time duration). In our case, we move to the 8 seconds mark. Then **move** the Hotair Balloon.psd (image 1) layer to any location on the Composition panel, as shown in picture 4.2.

You will see on your screen that a new keyframe is added at the 8 seconds mark on the timeline. You have animated a layer from position A to position B using the Position property.

Now let's animate the rotation of the layer using the Rotation property, which will make the animation more attractive.

4. Press the **Home key** on the keyboard to move the CTI to the start of the timeline. Then **click** the Time-Vary stop watch button for the Rotation property. You will see on your screen that a new keyframe is added for the Rotation property at the first frame in the timeline.

5. **Drag** the CTI to another frame (time duration). In our case, we move to the 4 seconds mark on the timeline.

6. Set any **Rotation value** in the Rotation property in the Timeline panel. In our case, we set the value to 30^0. You will see on your screen that a new keyframe is added for the Rotation property at the 4 seconds mark. This change is reflected on the Composition panel.

7. **Drag** the CTI to another frame or time duration. In our case, we move to the 8 seconds mark. Then **set** any Rotation value in the Timeline panel. In our case, we set the value to 0^0. Till now, we have added two keyframes to move the layer and three keyframes to rotate the layer. Now, let's preview the animation.

8. Press the **Home key** on the keyboard to move the CTI to the start of the timeline. Then press the **Spacebar key** to preview the animated layer transformation. As the result, you will see the balloon flying and rotating on your Composition panel.

Similarly, you can animate other Transformation properties, such as Anchor Point, Scale, and Opacity by changing their respective values over time. You can add multiple keyframes over different frames and change values to create complex animations.

Working with Motion Path

Besides the standard ways of accessing properties, motion paths provide an alternative way of accessing these properties and their keyframes. When you animate a layer property, such as Position and Rotation, motion path appears on the Composition panel. A motion path visually represents the movement of a layer. It appears as a sequence of small dots along a line, each dot representing the layer properties at each frame of an animation. The small squares in the path represent the position of keyframes. You can modify a motion path by changing an existing keyframe or adding keyframes. The density of small dots between the small squares in a motion path indicates the relative speed of the layer or effect control point.

The motion path appears on the Composition panel. You may need to adjust the zoom magnification to be able to see the motion path. You can set the zoom magnification level in the Magnification ratio popup dropdown list at the bottom of the Composition panel. The motion paths for the Position property appear on the Composition panel; whereas, for the Anchor Point and effect control point properties, motion paths appear in the Layer panel. To show motion path controls, you can select View> View Options from the Menu bar, and then select the Effect Controls, Keyframes, Motion Paths, and Motion Handles check boxes. Perform the following steps to modify an animation by changing the motion path:

1. **Select** a layer in the Timeline panel for which you want to modify the motion path. In our case, we select the animated hot air balloon.

2. Select a **keyframe** on the motion path. A keyframe on the motion path means the small square that you see on the doted line. In our case, we select the keyframe at the first frame which is at the bottom-left side in the Composition panel (shown in picture 4.3 with the red arrow on the left). When you select a keyframe, it appears as a solid square with a direction handle.

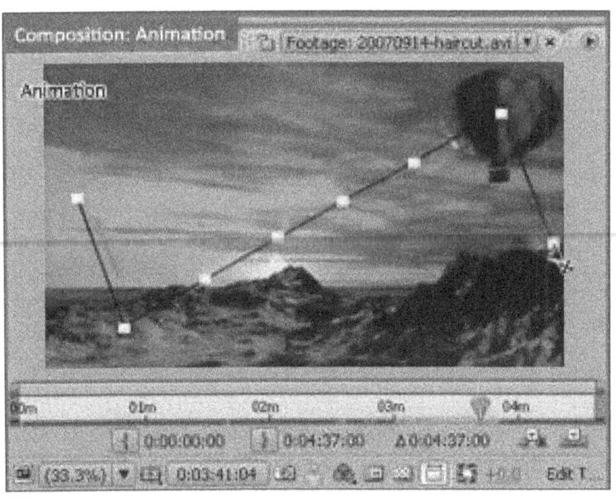

Picture 4.3

3. **Drag** the direction handle of the keyframe in any direction to modify the motion path. In our case, we dragged it anticlockwise (shown in picture 4.3).

4. **Select** another keyframe that you want to modify. In our case, we select the keyframe at the 8 seconds mark (top most keyframe). Then **drag** the direction handle of the keyframe to modify the motion path. We drag it anticlockwise (shown in picture 4.3).

5. **Preview** the animation with the modified motion path. You can observe that the hot air balloon moves in a wavy path instead of a straight line.

If you want, you can move the entire motion path by selecting all keyframes before dragging on the Composition panel. To select all the keyframes, click the property name in the Timeline panel. In addition to modifying keyframes, you can also add keyframes on the motion path using Pen Tool.

Animating 3D Layers

In After Effects, you can animate 3D layers by animating their properties, similar to 2D layers. You can enable the animation for a 3D property by clicking on the Time-Vary stop watch button on the left of the property. After you have enabled it, for every change, a new animation keyframe is created. You can change the numerical values for a property in the Timeline panel, or edit the layer directly in the Composition panel to change the property. However, while working with 3D layers, the Opacity property remains unchanged. Using the Orientation or Rotation properties, you can rotate a 3D layer by changing their values. However, these properties differ in the appearance of a layer after animating it. By default, when you rotate a 3D layer, it rotates around its anchor point. When you animate the Orientation property of a 3D layer, the layer rotates directly. However, when you animate any of the X, Y, or Z Rotation properties, the layer rotates along each individual axis. You can frequently animate the Orientation property for natural and smooth motions and animate the Rotation properties for more precise rotations. Perform these steps to animate a 3D layer by rotating it on the Composition panel:

Picture 4.4

1. **Select** a layer in the Timeline panel. In our case, we select the Car.mp4 layer, shown in picture 4.4. The video footage item is set against a black background of the composition.

2. Click the **3D Layer** layer-switch column for the Car.mp4 layer in the Timeline panel to convert it to a 3D layer. The picture of 3D Layer switch is already shown in picture 3.3.

3. **Expand** the Car.mp4 layer properties. Then click the **Time-Vary stop watch** button for the Orientation property.

It makes the animation feature enabled and a new keyframe is added for the Orientation property at the first frame of the timeline.

Picture 4.5

4. **Move** the CTI to the frame at 10 seconds mark. Then **set** the Orientation value for the Y-axis in the Timeline panel. In our case, we set it to 45^0. The 3D layer also rotates on the Composition panel, as shown in picture 4.5.

Alternatively, you can select Rotation Tool from the Tools panel, and select the Orientation option from the Set dropdown list on the Tools panel, and manually rotate the 3D layer. You can drag the selected axis in the Composition panel while holding the Shift key down to constrain the orientation to 45^0 increments.

5. Press the **Home key** to move the CTI to the start of the composition. Then preview the animation by pressing the **Spacebar** key.

Using Null Objects

In After Effects, null objects provide more control to work with layers. A null object is an invisible layer that includes all the transform properties of a visible layer. Null object layers can be used as helper objects; you can use them as a parent to any layer in the composition. Using a null object, you can combine all layers that you need to animate and make them children of the null object. For instance, you can parent multiple layers to a single null object layer; as you scale the null object layer, all the other layers scale, while maintaining their relationship to each other.

When you need to move multiple layers in a scene simultaneously, you can select all the layers and choose Layer> Pre-Compose from the Menu bar. However, if you need to access all those individual elements, as well as every other layer in the composition, you can create a null object. You can create a null object by selecting Layer> New> Null Object from the Menu bar. Null objects are always created with a width and height of 100 pixels. You can apply keyframes to the null object similar to pre-compositions or nested composition. Null objects do not control opacity value. Perform the following steps to transform multiple layers simultaneously using a null object:

1. **Select** the composition in which you want to use a null object to animate multiple layers. In our case, we select the Sky composition with multiple hot hair balloons to animate using a null object.

2. Select **Layer> New> Null Object** from the Menu bar to create a null object layer. A null object layer is created and displayed in the Timeline panel as well as in the Composition panel.

By default, null object layer is named Null 1. You can see the null object in the Composition panel of your screen as an empty bounding box. This represents the null object to help you keep track of it while working.

3. **Select** the 3D Layer layer-switch for the Null 1 layer to convert it into a 3D layer. The null object moves to the origin point of the composition (at the center of the grid).

4. **Select** the layers that you want to convert as children to the null object layer in the Timeline panel. In our case, we select four Hotair Balloon.psd layers.

5. **Select** the 1. Null 1 option from the Parent dropdown list for the Hotair Balloon.psd layer. 1. Null 1 is selected as the parent layer for the Hotair Balloon.psd layer; this is automatically applied to all the selected multiple layers. As the layers are now parented to the Null 1 layer, any changes to the null object also affect them.

6. **Select** the Null 1 layer in the Timeline panel and press the P key to reveal the Position property. Then **click** the Time-Vary stop watch button for the Null 1 layer. A new keyframe is added at the first frame.

7. **Move** the CTI to another frame (6 seconds mark). Then **set** the <u>Position</u> property as -170.0, to move all the hot air balloons upward. As the Hotair Balloon.psd layers are linked to the null object (Null 1), all the selected layers moved upward on the Composition panel.

8. Press the **Home key** to move the CTI to the first frame on the timeline. Then press the **Spacebar key** to preview the animation.

Animating Cameras

A camera allows you to see a composition from any angle. Cameras in After Effects are 3D layers that you can animate. To configure a camera to resemble the real-world camera, you can modify and animate camera settings in After Effects. Real-world cameras are used to record video footage to be used while compositing. Camera settings can also be used to add behaviors, such as depth of field blur, pans, dolly shots, synthetic effects, and animations. In After Effects, you can animate camera properties, such as Zoom, Depth of Field, Blur Level, and Focus Distance. Animating these properties is similar to animating other layer properties. Perform the following steps to animate a camera:

1. Select **Layer> New> Camera** from the Menu bar or press Ctrl+Alt+Shift+C keys together to create a camera.

2. **Expand** the <u>Camera Options</u> property group in the Timeline panel. You can see on your screen that the camera layer appears at the top of the stacking order, named Camera. In our case, the CTI is at the 2 seconds mark in the timeline.

3. Select the **2 Views – Horizontal** option from the <u>Select camera layout</u> dropdown list at the bottom of the Composition panel. The Composition panel displays two views, namely: Top and Active Camera.

4. **Click** the Time-Vary stop watch button for the property that you want to animate. In our case, we click the Time-Vary stop watch button for the Zoom property to add a keyframe at the CTI.

You can see on your screen that a keyframe is added at the 2 seconds mark in the timeline. You can also see that the Zoom property is at 1388.9 pixels (49.5°H), where H refers to Horizontal. The value in the bracket is automatically set when you modify the first value.

5. **Drag** the CTI to 8 seconds mark on the timeline. Then **set** a new Zoom property value. In our case, we set the Zoom property value as 2080.9 pixels (34.2^{0}H). You can see on your screen that a keyframe is added at the 8 seconds mark. You can also see the camera zooms in both Top and Active Camera view on the Composition panel.

6. Press the **Home key** to move the CTI to the start of the composition. Then press the **Spacebar key** to preview the animated camera. Similarly, you can animate other camera properties using keyframes for different cases.

Lesson 13
Working with Text

Text plays an integral part in communicating ideas irrespective of being a print design or a motion graphic design. The text animation capabilities of After Effects have made it as one popular application creating exciting text effects, such as animated titles, lower thirds, and credit rolls. Creating and editing text in After Effects is similar to Illustrator and Photoshop. To add text into a composition, select a type tool on the Tools panel, click anywhere on the Composition panel to add text, and then type the text. You can also convert text into a mask or a path outline. For instance, using the Create Masks from the Text command, you can extract each character's outline, create masks from the outlines, and place the masks on a new solid layer. You can also convert a text layer into a 3D layer and 3D sub-layers. After Effects CS6 has introduced the bevel and extrusion features for the 3D text layers. Using Bevel Style, Bevel Depth, and Extrusion Depth properties, you can modify the beveled and extruded text.

In After Effects, you can create both point and paragraph text. In the Character panel, you can set the text attributes either before or after adding text. Using the Character panel, you can set common text attributes, such as font family, font style, font size, and font color. When you add text into a composition, text layers are created, which are vector layers. Text layers retain crisp, resolution-independent edges when you scale or resize them. To create motion typography, you can animate text using the text animator properties, such as Offset, Shape, Blur, and Skew. You can animate properties of all text layers or the properties of individual characters. In this lesson, you first learn to create, format, and use text. Next, you learn to create text on a path. You also learn to animate text using a text animation preset as well as create a custom text animation. Towards the end, you also learn to work with 3D text.

Using Text in After Effects

In After Effects, you can create two types of text, namely: point text and paragraph text. Let's discuss the two types of text as follows:

Point text: Allows you to create a letter, single word, or sentence. To create point text, select a type tool, click on the Composition panel, and type a text. While typing, if you press the Enter key, a new line is created. Point text helps to create a title or other small text.

Paragraph text: Allows you to enter text as a paragraph. This type of text helps to fit text into a specific area in a composition. To create paragraph text, select a type tool, click and drag on the Composition panel to define an area, and then type a text. Unlike point text, in this type of text, a line of text automatically wraps to form new lines.

In addition to creating text, you can also copy text from other applications including Photoshop, Illustrator, and InDesign, and paste it into a text frame in After Effects. There are a wide range of text attributes that you can set using the Character and Paragraph panels. You can set formatting options for individual characters or entire paragraph including alignment, justification, and word-wrapping. Using the Character panel, you can set a specific font (font family), font style, font size, tracking, and kerning. By default, Times New Roman is selected as the font family and Regular is selected as the font style. If text is highlighted on the Composition panel, any changes in the Character panel affect only the highlighted text. In case no text is highlighted, changed affect the entire text layer or selected text layers. Note that, if no text is highlighted and no text layers are selected, the changes you make in the Character panel become the new default for the next text entry. You can also transform a text layer using properties in the Transform property group. By the way, tracking refers to adding an equal amount of spacing across a range of letters; kerning refers to increasing or decreasing the space between selected pair of letters.

Similarly, using the Paragraph panel, you can set properties for the paragraph text. Using the properties in the Paragraph panel, you can create automatic breaks between paragraphs, and align rows of text to the left, center, or right, or justify them to the margins. The baseline shifting feature allows you to raise or lower text off its original line. You can open the Character panel and Paragraph panel on your screen to view with their default settings in After Effects.

Creating Text using Type Tool

To create text in After Effects, use the type tools, namely: Horizontal Type Tool and Vertical Type Tool. You can access the type tools from the Tools panel. Horizontal Type Tool is selected by default and allows you to create both horizontal point and paragraph text. To create a point text, click and type on the Composition panel. To create a paragraph text, define a text frame by clicking and dragging on the Composition panel, and then type the text. Similarly, Vertical Type Tool allows you to create both vertical point and paragraph text. While typing a text, the basic editing features are available for use; for instance, pressing the Backspace key removes a letter. Perform the following steps to create text using the type tools:

1. **Select** a composition (in Project panel) in which you want to add a text. Then select **Horizontal Type Tool** from the Tools panel.

When you activate a type tool for the first time, the Character and Paragraph panels automatically appear in the workspace. Alternatively, select the Text workspace to display the Character and Paragraph panels. The Text workspace includes all panels that help you to create and manipulate text. To select the Text workspace, you need to select Window> Workspace> Text from the Menu bar, or select the Text option from the Workspace dropdown list on the Tools panel. By default, both the panels appear with the default settings. You can set text properties before or after you create a text. In our case, we have set the properties in the Character panel before creating the text.

2. **Select** a font fill color using the Fill Color swatch. In our case, we set the font fill color to white, as shown in picture 4.6 with the red arrow numbered 1.

3. **Select** a font stroke color using the Stroke Color swatch. In our case, we set the font stroke color to none, as shown in picture 4.6 with the red arrow numbered 2.

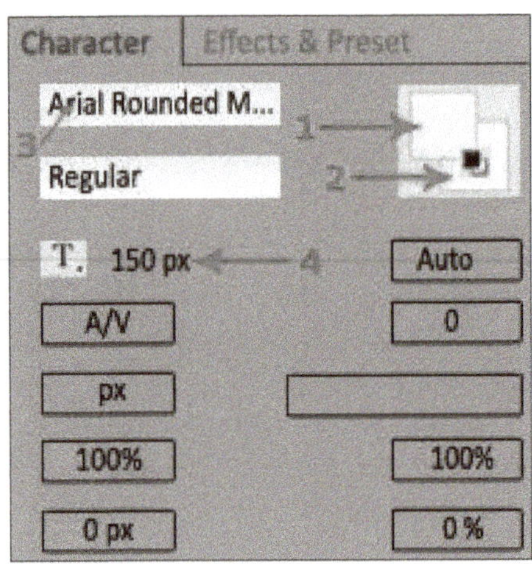

Picture 4.6

4. Select a **font family**. In our case, we select Arial Rounded MT Bold from the <u>Set the font family</u> dropdown list, as shown in picture 4.6 with the red arrow numbered 3.

5. **Set** any font size in the <u>Set the font size</u> option, shown in picture 4.6 with the red arrow numbered 4. Then **move** the <u>Horizontal Type Tool</u> cursor over any area to add a text on the Composition panel.

6. **Click on** the Composition panel to activate the text insertion mode and **type** a text to add it. In our case, we type: **Signatures**. By the way, while adding point text, you can press the Enter key to add multiple lines.

7. **Deactivate** Horizontal Type Tool to exit text insertion mode. To deactivate a type tool, select any other tool or a layer in the Timeline panel.

Similarly, to create a paragraph text, define a text frame for the text using the type tool cursor and then type a text. The paragraph text automatically breaks on reaching the edge to form new lines without exceeding the width of the text frame. While doing so, the text layers are automatically created in the Timeline panel. Note that the Character and Paragraph panels retain the last settings that you can use to create or edit the text. It is usually referred to set the initial properties before you create the text.

Formatting the Text

Formatting allows you to control the appearance of individual characters or the whole text. Mostly, after creating a text, you have to format it. To format a text, you can use the text attributes in the Character panel or Paragraph panel. You can edit text properties, such as font family, size, style, and color in the Character panel to format a text. You can also format text using the Timeline panel. The text that you create is placed on a separate layer in the Timeline panel. It is called as the Source Text. Each text layer contains two property groups, namely: Text and Transform. In After Effects, it is easy to try different text formatting in a composition, by easily adjusting the text properties as required. While formatting text, changing one value (font size) might call for changing other values, such as leading, tracking, or kerning, to maintain the readability of the text. Perform the following steps to format a text:

1. **Double-click** a text layer that you want to format in the Timeline panel. This selects all the text on the Composition panel. In other case, if you want to add words to the selection, you need to hold the Shift key down, and double-click any word with a type tool to select it.

2. Click the **Fill Color** swatch button in the <u>Character panel</u>, select a **color** as the text color from the Text Color dialog box, and then click the **OK** button.

3. Change the **Set the tracking** for the selected characters value to **10**. If you want to change a property value, you need to drag the underlined value for the property.

4. Change the **Set the stroke width** value to **10 px**. Then **select** a stroke width type from the **Set the stroke width** dropdown list. In our case, we select **Stroke Over Fill**.

5. **Set** the font size using the **Set the font size** property. In our case, we set it to 180 px. Font size specifies the size of the text in pixels. Simultaneously, the highlighted text on the Composition panel reflects the changes.

6. **Select** another tool or layer to deselect the highlighted text. The text appears formatted on your screen.

You can also click and drag the type tool over a letter or a word to highlight it and then change its properties to create interesting type effects. When active inside a text frame, the cursor allows you to select any number of characters, words, or lines. The changes made in the Character or Paragraph panel affect only the highlighted text.

Creating Outline from Text

In After Effects, text layers are vector layers that can be converted into vector shapes or outlines. Using the Create Shapes from Text command under the Layer menu, you can convert a text layer into vector outlines. It extracts the outlines for each character and creates shapes from each outline. This command also creates a new shape layer for each shape. You can then use these shapes to modify or animate as required. You can modify the shape outlines using Convert Vertex Tool. Using font families such as Webdings, you can create simple graphical elements in shape layers. Webdings include characters that are graphical images, rather than text. Perform the following steps on your computer to create outlines from text:

1. **Select** a text that you want to convert to outlines. In our case, we select Signatures text that we had created in previous section.

2. Choose **Layer> Create Shapes from Text** from the Menu bar. The highlighted text on the Composition panel is converted to outlines. If you want to create shapes for specific characters, you need to highlight them on the Composition panel.

As you can see on your screen that the selected text is converted to shapes and a new layer is created in the Timeline panel. The new shape layer is created at the top of the layer stacking order. The shape layer includes Contents and Transform property groups. Using the Contents property group, you can modify individual shapes and animate them; using the Transform property group, you can transform the properties of the layer as a whole. In the Contents property group, several groups representing each individual character are created. Each group further contains one shape group for each selected character. In addition, it contains the Fill and Stroke properties that resemble the fills and strokes of the text. For characters that consist of compound paths, such as 'i' and 'e', multiple paths are created and combined using the Merge Paths path operation.

You can modify every shape and animate its properties. When you modify any of the properties, a keyframe is added at the Current Time Indicator (CTI). You can animate the Path, Fill, Stroke, and Transform properties of the individual shape separately to create text animations. By the way, when you select the Create Shapes from Text option, the Video switch for the text layer is turned off automatically. Now in the next section, we will learn to create masks from text which is quite fascinating in After Effects CS6.

Creating Mask from Text

In After Effects, you can create masks from text by selecting Layer> Create Masks from Text from the Menu bar. This command extracts the text outlines from each character as shapes, and then creates masks from the shapes and places them on a new solid layer. You can then modify the shape of the masks using Convert Vertex Tool. Perform the following steps to create masks from text:

Picture 4.7

1. **Select** the text that you want to convert as a text mask. We select the CAR layer in a new composition, which also contains the Car.mp4 video layer.

2. Select **Layer> Create Masks from Text** from the Menu bar. Alternatively, you can right-click the layer in the Timeline panel or text on the Composition panel, and then select the Create Masks from Text option from the context menu. A new solid layer (CAR Outlines) is created at the top of the layer stacking order and the fill color of the text changes to white representing the opaque area, as shown in picture 4.7.

The solid layer includes a separate layer for each character in the text. If the character consist of compound paths, such as 'a' and 'e', multiple layers are created in the Timeline panel. In our case, the

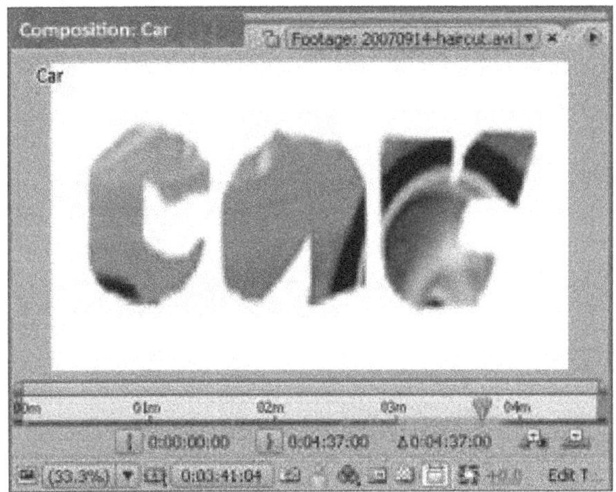

Picture 4.8

character has two layers. Each individual layer contains mask properties, such as Mask Path, Mask Feather, Mask Opacity, and Mask Expansion that you can use to modify and animate the mask.

3. In the Timeline, **click** the check box of the name Inverted for any of the individual mask. In our case, we click the Inverted check box for **layer C**.

This creates the mask effect in After Effects CS6. The area inside the mask becomes transparent revealing the layer beneath it, as shown in picture 4.8. Let's now learn to create text on path.

Creating Text on Path

In After Effects, you can create text on a path by combining it with mask paths. When a text is masked, it can follow the mask as path. You can modify the path any time after creating it. You can animate the text along that path and animate the path as well. You can use either the open mask or the closed mask to create paths for text. If you use a closed mask as a text path, you need to set the mask mode to None. You can select the name of the mask in the Path Options property group in the Timeline panel. When text on a path is created, the following five properties appear for the path option:

Reverse Path: Reverses the direction of a path. When a path is drawn in the wrong direction, the text appears backwards. This property allows you to override the default positioning of the path. By default, this option is Off.

Perpendicular to Path: Rotates each character to make it perpendicular to the path. By default, it is horizontal to the path.

Force Alignment: Positions the first character at the beginning of the path and the last character at the end of the path, and evenly spaces the remaining characters between the first and last characters. By default, this option is Off.

First Margin: Specifies the position of the first character relative to the start of the path. By default, this option is set to 0.0.

Last Margin: Specifies the position of the last character relative to the end of the path. By default, this option is set to 0.0. Now perform the following steps to create a text on a path:

1. **Select** a text layer in the Timeline panel to create a text on a path. In our case, we have selected **Creating text**.

2. **Create** a mask path using shape tools or Pen Tool. In our case, we create an elliptical shape using Ellipse Tool, as shown in picture 4.9. In case a mask pat is already on the text layer, it is automatically activated when you select the text layer.

Picture 4.9

Picture 5.0

3. In the Timeline panel, **click** the **dropdown arrow on the left to the layer name** while holding Ctrl key down to expand all the property groups. It adds a mask layer (Mask 1) when you create a mask path.

4. **Select** a mask path from the <u>Path</u> dropdown list. In our case, we select Mask 1. As the result, the text appears on the mask path on the Composition panel, as shown in picture 5.0.

Lesson 14
Animating Text

In After Effects, there are several ways to animate text layers, namely: manually creating keyframes in the Timeline panel, using animation presets, or using expressions. There is an advantage in using animation presets, it allows you to reuse animations and tweak them instead of creating everything from scratch. You can also animate individual characters or words in a text layer. Text layers provide additional animation features that help to animate a text within the layers to create flexible and complex animations in a very short duration. You can select Animation> Browse Presets from the Menu bar and double-click the Text folder in the Adobe Bridge application to access various animation presets. Adobe Bridge is a stand-alone application that allows you to browse and preview media files and animation presets. This application is installed when you install the Adobe Creative Suite from the Adobe software CD.

Text layers have two types of properties, namely: Transform and Text animators. Transform properties are applied on any layer; text animators are applied on only text layers. Text animators contain both the Text and the Range Selector properties. The first set of properties is the standard set, such as Anchor Point, Position, Rotation, Scale, and Opacity. The second set of properties is animators, such as Offset and Mode, available only for a text layer. A list of Text properties are discussed as follows:

Anchor Point: Sets the anchor point for characters. Anchor point is the origin point for any type of transformations.
Position: Specifies the X and Y positions of a text in relation to the composition size.
Rotation, X Rotation, Y Rotation, Z Rotation: Specifies the rotation of each character on a text layer that you enter.
Scale: Specifies the horizontal and vertical scale of characters.
Skew: Distorts a text by rotating its individual characters.
All Transformation Properties: Adds all transformation properties to the animator group, simultaneously.
Line Anchor: Specifies the point of alignment for tracking in a line of text. A value of 0 percent is left alignment, 50 percent is center alignment, and 100 percent is right alignment.
Line Spacing: Specifies the space between lines or leading value.
Character Offset: Specifies the amount of offset of characters in a text layer. You can use this property to shift characters in a text layer to form random words.
Characters Value: Replaces all characters in a word as per the selected value amount.
Blur: Sets the amount for Gaussian blurs.

Let's now discuss the Range Selector properties, as given below:
Start and End: Specifies the beginning and end of a selection.
Offset: Specifies the amount of offset from the current position of the Start and End points of the range selectors.
Shape: Sets the character selection between the Start and End points of the range selector.
Mode: Specifies the combination of each selector with a text and the selector above it, to create an effect similar to combination of multiple masks after applying a mask mode property.
Amount: Controls the strength of an animator's effect, and sets the amount of range of characters to be affected by the animator properties.
Units and Based On: Serves as the unit of measure for the Start, End, and Offset properties.
Smoothness: Sets the amount of time the animation takes to transition from one character to another. Higher numbers produce soft transitions.
Ease High and Ease Low: Determines the speed of change as selection values change from fully included (high) to fully excluded (low). For instance, when the Ease High option is set to 100%, the character changes more gradually (eases into the change), fully to partially selected.
Randomize Order: Organizes the order randomly for applying its properties to characters. Let's begin with animating text using a text animation preset.

Using a Text Animation Preset

Text animation presets are built-in animations that you can apply on a text layer in After Effects. These presets help new users to work with text animations. You can use the text animation presets in the Effects & Presets panel or browse for them in the Adobe Bridge application. Each preset remains fully editable after you apply them on text, which allows you to apply as well as modify these effects as required. Perform the following steps to animate a text using a text animation preset:

1. **Select** a text layer in the Timeline panel. In our case, we select the **SIGNATURE** layer. In case you want to reveal the entire layer name, you need to drag the Layer name column using the dividers that separate each column's name.

2. Select **Animation> Browse Presets** from the Menu bar to open the Adobe Bridge application. Adobe Bridge opens with the default Presets folder after a few seconds.

3. Double-click the **Text folder** to display the text animation presets. The Text folder includes different categories of text animation presets.

4. Double-click the **Organic folder** to display the text animation presets for this category. It opens several text animation presets for the Organic category. Before applying an animation preset, you can preview it in Adobe Bridge. To preview an animation preset, just **select** it. The PREVIEW section plays the preset in a loop.

5. **Right-click** the Drop Bounce.ffx animation preset, and **select** the Place In After Effects option from the context menu.

The .ffx extension is used to save animation presets in After Effects. As animation presets were previously called favorite effects, the file extension is .ffx. The After Effects interface reappears and the animation preset is automatically applied to the selected layer in the Timeline panel. The text may disappear on the Composition panel; however, the animation appears when you preview it.

6. Press the **Spacebar** key to preview the text animation. Alternatively, you can double-click an animation preset to apply it to a selected layer. However, ensure that a layer is selected before applying a preset. In case, no layer is selected in the Timeline panel, a new text layer is created and the preset is applied on the layer.

Creating Custom Text Animation

As discussed earlier, using text animation presets, you can easily create text animations in After Effects. You can also customize an animation preset by adjusting its properties in the Timeline panel and create customized text animations. A simple adjustment to these properties can completely change the nature and appearance of the animation. You can also save a custom text animation preset using the Animation> Save Animation Preset option from the Menu bar. You can also work with third-party animation presets other than the built-in presets.

Alternatively, you can use text animator groups to animate the properties of individual characters in a text layer over time. Text animator groups contain one or more selectors similar to masks. Using selectors, you can specify the characters or section of a text layer to be affected by an animator property. Using a selector, you can define a percentage of a text, specific characters in a text, or a specific range of text. For instance, you can create a custom text animation by creating a typewriter effect. In this effect, text appears on the screen one letter at a time creating a typing effect. You can later save the text animation as a text animation preset. Perform the following steps to create a typewriter effect:

1. **Create** a text layer. In our case, we create a text layer containing the text: Old Mumbai Street. If required, you can format the text by highlighting it.

2. **Expand** the text layer in the Timeline panel. Then **click** the dropdown arrow on the right of the Animate menu for the Text property. It opens a dropdown list with various animator groups.

3. Select the **Opacity** option from the dropdown list to add a new animator group to the layer. It opens a new animator group along with a default selector and the chosen animator property in the Timeline panel. Alternatively, to add an animator group, select Animation> Animate Text from the Menu bar, and then select a property from the submenu for the selected text layer.

4. **Set** the Opacity property to 0% by dragging the underlined value towards the left. By default, the Opacity value is set to 100%. When you change the Opacity value to 0%, the text disappears from the Composition panel.

5. Expand the **Range Selector 1** group to display its properties. Then click **the Time-Vary stop watch** button of the Start property to add a keyframe for the property at the CTI. A new keyframe is added at the CTI. By default, the value of the Start property of a range selector is 0% and the value of the End property of a range selector is 100%.

When you create a new project or composition, the CTI or (playhead) appears at the start of the Timeline. Press the Home key to move the playhead to the start of the Timeline. When the playhead is at the beginning of the timeline, the Current Time displays 0;00;00;00.

6. **Move** the playhead to the next frame to add the next keyframe. In our case, we move it to 0;00;37;15 on the timeline. Then **change** the Start property value to 100%. This makes the text (Old Mumbai Street) reappear on the Composition panel and a new keyframe is added.

7. **Preview** the custom animation. To preview, drag the playhead (CTI) to scroll the animation forward and backward. You can see that while previewing the animation, the letters in the text appear individually. However, the letters seem to fade in as opposed to the on/off effect with the typewriter effect. Let's proceed to fine tune the custom animation.

8. Expand the Advanced property group for **Range Selector 1**. Then change the **Smoothness** value to 0%. By default, the Smoothness value is set to 100%. This eliminates the fading effect completely from the animation.

9. **Preview** the text animation. You can see the typewriter effect animation plays between the two keyframes without the fade in effect. You can save the custom text animation as a preset and apply it on different text layers. Select Animation> Save Animation Preset from the Menu bar to save the text animation as a preset.

By the way, if the playhead is not currently on a keyframe, then the Add or remove keyframe at the current time button appears gray. To add a new keyframe at the playhead position, click this button when it is gray. You can remove the existing keyframe at the playhead position when it is yellow.

Working with 3D Text

Text layers are similar to any other layer in After Effects. Hence, you can convert a normal text layer into a 3D layer by activating the 3D Layer switch. This enables you to manipulate the layer with three dimensions. When you convert a layer to 3D, additional properties such as Position (Z), Anchor Point (Z), Scale (Z), Orientation, X Rotation, Y Rotation, Z Rotation, and Material Options, appear for the layer in the Timeline panel. The Material Options properties specify the interaction of the layer with lights, shadows, and cameras. You can also apply effects and expressions to 3D text layers, animate and edit them while viewing it in multiple views. However, you cannot open text in its own Layer panel. You can animate the text in a text layer using special text animator properties and selectors. A text layer automatically becomes a 3D layer when you enable 3D properties for its characters. Hence, a text layer becomes a 3D layer when a per-character 3D property is added to it, by applying a 3D Text animation preset. Perform the following steps to create a 3D text in After Effects CS6:

1. **Select** a text layer. In our case, we select a layer containing the text CAR which we had created in previous lesson.

2. Click the **3D Layer switch** for the CAR layer in the Timeline panel. It converts the two dimensional (2D) layer to a 3D layer. The 3D Layer switch icon as well as the 3D axis gizmo appears. Now we can transform the 3D text layer.

3. Select **Rotation Tool** on the Tools panel and **move** the mouse-pointer above the green color axis (Y-axis); this axis appears when you convert a layer into 3D layer.

4. **Click and drag** the Y-axis of the 3D axes to rotate the 3D layer. In our case, we drag the Y-axis towards right to rotate the 3D text layer. Alternatively, you can use the Orientation property in the Timeline panel to rotate the 3D layer.

Similarly, you can edit the 3D text layer by modifying various properties, such as Anchor Point, Position, Scale, and Opacity. In addition, you can animate these properties using keyframes. You can also add text animation presets. Let's proceed to add a 3D text animation preset reflection to the CAR 3D layer.

5. Select **Animation> Browse Presets** from the Menu bar to open the Adobe Bridge application. Then double-click the **Text folder** to display the text animation presets. The Text folder includes different categories of text animation presets.

6. Double-click the **3D Text folder** to display the text animation presets for this category. It displays several text animation presets for the 3D Text category.

7. Right-click the **3D Flip Up Reflection.ffx** animation preset and select the **Place In After Effects** option from the context menu. Then press the **Spacebar** key to preview the text animation. You can also cast shadows on 3D layers as in the real world, where objects cast reflections in certain lighting environment adding depth.

Lesson 15
Working with Masks, Track Mattes, and Chroma Keys
After Effects is known for its capabilities for seamless compositing of video shots using transparency. For this, different techniques such as masks, track mattes, and Chroma keys are available. Masks are vector paths that you can use to hide or reveal part of a layer. By default, the selected portion of a layer is revealed and the unselected portion is hidden. You can also modify this behavior using the Inverted option. The unselected portion of a layer is protected from editing. Using the frame-by-frame method, you can also animate a mask to monitor the movement of an object in a composition.

Track mattes are layers and are similar to masks. However, the procedure of creating transparency using track mattes is different from masks. Unlike masks that use vector paths to isolate areas of layer, track mattes use either alpha (transparency) or luminance (brightness). In a track matte, white represents opaque areas and black represents transparent areas. Although, both techniques are useful for creating transparency and merging multiple layers, they consume a lot of time while working with a video, as the subject often changes its position. For such cases, you can use another technique called Chroma key. This key uses a particular color value or luminance value to create transparency by removing one color. This technique is very popular while merging green or blue screen live action footage to a computer generated (CG) footage. In this chapter, you learn to create a mask using the shape tools as well as Pen Tool, edit a mask path, create a vignette effect, and animate a mask. You also learn to use Mask Feather Tool. Next, you learn to work with track mattes to create transparency. In addition, you learn about Chroma keying technique, which includes creating a garbage matte, creating a Chroma key, and refining a matte. Towards the end, you learn to use the Hue/Saturation effect to color correct a video footage.

Working with Masks
Masks are vector-based paths or outlines used to hide or reveal portions of an image. They are also used to modify layer effects and properties. You can create masks from simple primitive shapes, such as rectangles and circles, import them from vector-based drawing program, such as Adobe Illustrator, or create them in After Effects using the shape tools or Pen Tool. The most common use of a mask is to modify the alpha channel of a layer, which determines its transparency. Similar to a shape, a mask consists of segments and vertices. A mask can also be either an open or a closed path. An open path has a starting point and an ending point; for instance, a straight line is an open path. A closed path is a continuous path without any start or end points, such as a circle.

You can draw a mask directly in the Composition panel as well as in the Layer panel using the shape tools or Pen Tool. When you draw a mask using these tools, a vector path is created called as a mask path. By default, the area outside the mask path is transparent and shows the content of the layer beneath the masked layer; however, the area inside the mask path is opaque. You can also invert the display of opaque and transparent area using the Inverted option in the Timeline panel. In addition, you can also display the mask path without hiding any portion using the Layer panel. Unlike shape layers, a mask is created within a selected layer and belongs to that specific layer. In After Effects, a single layer can contain multiple masks. In Timeline, each mask layer may have four properties, namely: Mask Path, Mask Feather, Mask Opacity, and Mask Expansion. Following list describes the four properties of mask:

Mask Path: Specifies the position of the points (vertices) that constructs the mask. Using this property, you can animate the points to create an effect of a mask moving around a layer or to change the shape of the mask.

Mask Feather: Specifies the softness of the edge of a mask and creates the effect of a layer fading into a background. By default, the feather width overlaps the mask edge; for instance, if you set the feather width to 25 pixels, the feathering extends 12.5 pixels inside the mask edge and 12.5 pixels outside it.

Mask Opacity: Determines the influence that that a closed mask has on the alpha channel of the layer inside the mask area. A Mask Opacity value of 100% results in completely opaque mask area. The area outside the mask is always completely transparent.

Mask Expansion: Expands or contracts the area influenced by a mask. This property affects the alpha channel, but not the underlying mask path.

Masks are used to control the transparency of layers. The first mask you create affects the alpha channel of a layer, and any additional masks created interact with the masks above it in the stacking order. In addition to the four properties, each mask also has a mode setting that controls its interaction with the mask above it. You can access these mask modes in the Timeline panel. The modes of a mask are discussed as follows:

None: Allows you to use a mask path for effects, such as Stroke and Fill, or use a mask path as the base for a shape path. With this mode selected, the mask has no direct influence on the alpha channel of the layer.

Add: Combines the transparency values of a mask that overlaps the same layer. By default, this mask mode is selected.

Subtract: Subtracts the transparency values of a mask that overlaps the same layer. This mode hides everything inside the mask if it is the only mask on that layer.

Intersect: Adds a selected mask to the masks above it in the stacking order. When all masks in a layer are set to the Intersect mode, only those areas formed by overlapping these masks are visible.

Lighten: Adds a selected mask to the masks above it in the stacking order. When multiple masks intersect, the highest Mask Opacity value is used for overlapping areas.

Darken: Adds a selected mask to the masks above it in the stacking order. When multiple masks intersect, the lowest Mask Opacity value is used for overlapping areas.

Difference: Adds a selected mask to the masks above it in the stacking order. When using multiple masks, which do not overlap, masks seem to have been set to the Add mode. When the mask overlaps with the masks above it, it seems to have been set to the Subtract mode.

Creating a Mask using a Shape Tool

To create a mask using a shape tool, select the shape tool from the Tools panel and then drag the shape on the Composition panel or the Layer panel. Shape tools, such as Rectangle Tool, Ellipse Tool, and Polygon Tool help you to create masks in predefined shapes. However, using Pen Tool, you can create Bezier shaped masks. Normally, drawing masks paths is similar to drawing shape paths. When you select a shape tool, you can specify whether the tool draws a shape or mask. Use the Tool Creates Mask and Tool Creates Shape buttons on the Tools panel to specify whether you want to create a shape or mask. Creating a mask or shape depends on the following rules:

- A mask is created if a non-shape layer is selected in the Timeline panel.
- A new shape layer is created if no layer is selected in the Timeline panel.
- If a shape layer is selected, the Tool Creates Shape and Tool Creates Mask buttons determine whether the shape tools and Pen Tool create a mask or a new shape path.

You can click in the Composition or Layer panel to start drawing and release the mouse button to stop drawing. Similarly, while drawing a mask, press the modifier keys at varying times to get different outputs, which are listed as follows:

- Hold the Spacebar key down on the keyboard while dragging the mouse cursor to reposition a shape or mask, while drawing.
- Hold the Ctrl key down while dragging the mouse cursor to scale a circle, ellipse, square, rounded square, rectangle, or rounded rectangle around its center, while drawing and release the key after completing the drawing.
- Press the Spacebar key on the keyboard to cancel the drawing the drawing anytime. Now you can perform the following steps to draw a mask using a shape tool:

1. **Create** a composition in which you want to create a mask using a shape tool. In our case, we create the Mask composition containing the Mask.mp4 video layer, as shown in picture 5.1.

To open a composition, double-click the composition name in the Project panel. When you double-click, the composition appears both in the Composition and Timeline panels. You can create a new composition based on the dimensions and length of the footage, by dragging it onto the Create a new Composition button at the bottom of the Project panel.

Picture 5.1   Picture 5.2

2. **Select** a layer on which you want to create a mask. In our case, we select the Mask.mp4 layer. Then **select** a shape tool from the Tools panel. In our case, we select Ellipse Tool.

3. **Click and drag** on the Composition panel to create a mask on the active layer, as shown in picture 5.2. As you can see in this picture as well as on your screen, the area outside the elliptical shape appears black. A mask property group is added below the selected layer in the Timeline panel. By default, the new mask is named Mask 1; however, to rename a mask, right-click the mask and select the Rename option. Similarly, you can draw masks using other shape tools.

Creating a Mask using Pen Tool

Shape tools are useful to create masks in uniform shapes. However, due to their inability to follow a specific contour, Pen Tool became one of the most powerful tools to create masks with contour. In After Effects, Pen Tool creates free form vector mask paths that hide or reveal areas of a layer. Using this tool, you can create vertices such as corner points or Bezier points to form straight lines or Bezier curves. You can also create a Bezier mask using Pen Tool on a selected layer in the Composition or Layer panel. When Pen Tool is selected, the Roto Bezier option appears in the Tools panel. Using this option, you can create Bezier curved mask paths automatically. The RotoBezier paths do not have Bezier handles; instead, a smooth path between the vertices is automatically calculated. Perform the following steps to create a mask using Pen Tool:

1. **Select** a layer onto which you want to create a mask using Pen Tool. In our case, we have selected Car.mp4 layer.

2. Select **Pen Tool** from the Tools panel or press the G key on the keyboard. Then **move** the Pen Tool cursor where you want the path to begin and **click** to place a vertex.

As you can see on your screen, the inserted vertex appears as a solid box. Just clicking inserts a corner point vertex as in our case. To insert a Bezier point vertex, click and drag on the layer. Similarly, you ca create multiple vertices by clicking and dragging on the layer.

3. **Move** the cursor to a different location to add the second vertex. Then **click** to insert the second vertex. You will see on your screen that a straight line appears connecting the first and second vertices.

4. **Move** the cursor to the location where you want to add the third vertex. Then **click** to insert the third vertex. Similarly, you can add multiple vertices to create a shape.

5. **Click** the first vertex to create a closed path. The area outside the mask path is automatically hidden. This reveals the layer beneath it. In our case, the underneath video layer appears outside the mask path.

While working in the Composition panel, you can hold the Spacebar key down on the keyboard to activate Hand Tool temporarily, irrespective of any other tool selected. Using Hand Tool, you can pan in the Composition panel.

The Mask 1 property group also appears in the Timeline panel. By default, the mask path shows to masked layer. You can invert the mask to show the underneath layer inside the mask path using the Inverted option. By default, the Inverted option is disabled.

6. In the Timeline panel, select the **Inverted** check box to swap the display of opaque and transparent areas. Then press the **Spacebar** key to preview the Mask.mp4 video inside the mask path.

Editing a Mask Path

In After Effects, editing a mask path is similar to editing a shape path. After creating a mask path, you may want to edit its shape as preferred. To edit the shape of a mask, adjust individual vertices of the mask path. Using Selection Tool, you can adjust the entire mask path as well as the position of each vertex. In addition to Selection Tool, you can use tools, such as Add Vertex Tool, Delete Vertex Tool, and Convert Vertex Tool to edit a mask path. Editing a mask path also involves adding more vertices or removing unnecessary vertices as required. Add Vertex Tool allows you to add new vertices; Delete Vertex Tool allows you to remove existing vertices; and Convert Vertex Tool allows you to convert a corner point to a smooth (Bezier) point.

By adding vertices to a mask path, you can make complex curves, corners, and bends. In a Bezier mask path, the positions of the direction lines and points determine the size and shape of the mask path. You can click an existing vertex to reset a curve, or click and drag the vertices to change the curve. You must ensure that the Toggle Mask and Shape Path Visibility button at the bottom of the Composition panel is enabled to view masks and shape paths in the Composition panel. Now in subsequent sections, you learn to change the default color for the mask outline, set the opacity of a mask, expand or contract the edge of a mask, and create the vignette effect. Let's begin by changing the mask outline color.

Changing the Mask Outline Color

The default color of a mask is yellow, which at times might not be visible against a background. In such case, you can change the color of the mask outline to make it visible against a background. The small color swatch button on the left of the mask name in Timeline panel lets you change the color of the mask outline. It represents the color of the selected mask. Perform the following steps to change the color of the mask outline:

1. **Select** a layer containing a mask in the Timeline panel, and press the **M key** to reveal the mask properties.

2. **Click** the color swatch button on the left of the mask name. It opens the Mask Color dialog box. Then select a color (red) for the mask outline.

3. Click the **OK** button to close the Mask Color dialog box. In the Composition panel, the color of the mask outline changes to red. You can see that the color swatch button in the Timeline panel turns red.

Setting Mask Opacity

In After Effects, masks are vector paths used as a parameter to modify layer attributes, effects, and properties. By default, the area inside a mask path is opaque and the area outside a mask path is completely transparent. You can control the opacity of the area inside a mask path. Using the Mask Opacity property for a mask, you can change its opacity. By default, the Mask Opacity value is set to 100%. Reducing the Mask Opacity value makes a mask less transparent. At 0% Mask Opacity value, a mask becomes completely opaque. Perform the following steps to change the opacity for a mask:

1. **Select** a layer in the Timeline panel containing a mask and press the **M key** twice in quick succession to display all mask properties. You can see on your screen that the mask path color is red in the Composition panel because we have changed it in previous section.

2. **Click** the underlined numeric value for the Mask Opacity property. A text box is temporarily activated. Then **type** the value: **20** in the Mask Opacity text box.

3. **Press** the Enter key on the keyboard or click anywhere outside the text box to accept the value. The Mask Opacity value becomes 20% and the area inside the mask appears to be semi-transparent.

4. Select the **Inverted** check box to make the area outside the mask path semi-transparent. In the next section, you learn about expanding or contracting a mask.

Expanding or Contracting a Mask

After creating a mask, you can expand or contract the edge of the mask path. The area influenced by a mask increases on expanding the edge, and decreases on contracting the edge. You can use the Mask Expansion property in the Timeline panel to expand or contract the edge of a mask. A negative Mask Expansion value contracts the area of influence, while a positive value expands the area of influence of a mask. Mask expansion only affects the alpha channel or the transparency, but not the underlying mask path. The mask expansion is essentially an offset that determines the extent a mask path influences a mask on the alpha channel. The Mask Expansion value is calculated in pixels. Perform the following steps to expand or contract a mask path:

1. **Select** the mask layer in the Timeline panel of your After Effects screen. Then you need to **expand** the Mask 1 property.

2. **Set** the Mask Expansion property in the Timeline panel to 60. The area influenced by the mask grows on the Composition panel.

You can see on your screen that the mask adds more transparent areas. Similarly, you can type a negative value (-20) to contract the transparent area defined by the mask path. After entering the negative value, the transparency is reduced while the original path remains the same, and only the influenced area is adjustable.

Changing the Shape of a Mask Path

There are different ways to modify or fine tune a mask path after creating it. However, if you want to completely change a custom mask path into either a rectangle or an ellipse, you can use the Mask Path option for the layer containing the mask. To reset the shape of a rectangle or an ellipse, click the Shape option and open the Mask Shape dialog box. You can also use this dialog box to reposition an entire mask path on the composition. Perform the following steps on your computer to change the shape of a mask path:

1. **Select** the layer containing a mask and **expand** its properties. In our case, we have selected and expanded Signature.mp4 layer.

2. Click the **Shape** option for the Mask Path property. It opens the Mask Shape dialog box. Then select the **Reset To** check box in the Shape section.

3. Select **Ellipse** option from the Reset To dropdown list. Then click the **OK** button to close the dialog box. You can see on your screen that the mask path changes into an ellipse.

Creating a Vignette Effect

A vignette effect is often added to footage to attract attention towards the center of it. It reduces the brightness and saturation at the periphery as compared to the center of the footage. The vignette effect is a popular effect in motion graphic design. Using the Mask Feather and Mask Expansion properties, you can create this vignette effect. You can apply a vignette effect to any composition in an After Effects project. This is often done to simulate light variations that focus attention on the subject. Perform the following steps to create a vignette effect:

1. **Select** a layer in the Timeline panel on which you want to create a vignette effect. In our case, we have selected the Car.mp4 layer.

2. Choose **Layer> New> Solid** from the Menu bar to create a solid layer above the selected layer. It opens the Solid Settings dialog box on the screen.

3. **Click** the color swatch in the Color section and **select** a color (royal blue) in the Solid Color dialog box. The name appears in the Name text box when you select a color by default.

4. Click the **OK** button to create a solid layer. By default, the solid layer is of the same size as the composition. To ensure composition size of the solid layer, click the Make Comp Size button. As the result, the new solid layer appears above the current selected layer in the Timeline panel as well as the Composition panel.

5. Select **Ellipse Tool** from the Tools panel. Then **double-click** the Ellipse Tool to create an ellipse with similar dimensions of the composition properties.

6. Expand the **Masks** properties by clicking the arrow on the left side of the mask name in the Timeline panel.

7. Select **Subtract** from the Blending Modes dropdown list for Mask 1. The mask appears inverted in the Composition panel. By the way, you can soften the effect of feather by adjusting the Mask Expansion property, which represents the original mask edge you are expanding or contracting.

8. **Expand** the Mask 1 property. Then you need to **set** the Mask Feather value to 140.0, 140.0 in the Timeline panel.

Keep in mind that the Constrain Proportions option, which is enabled by default, allows you to set the X and Y dimensions simultaneously. You can also set the X and Y values separately by disabling the Constrain Proportions option.

9. **Set** the Mask Expansion value to **30.0** in the Timeline panel. By the way, to set a property value, you can click an underlined value for a property and type a new value in the text box that appears temporarily. As the result, the vignette effect applies to the mask edge in the Composition panel.

Animating a Mask

Animating mask paths and shape paths in After Effects is similar to other applications. You can animate a mask path by modifying its properties or individual vertices over time. The changes are automatically interpolated to create a smooth blending of different mask paths. When you animate properties by setting keyframes for the Mask Path property, values between these specified values are interpolated. The Mask Path property stores the position of all individual vertices in a mask. Perform the following steps to animate a mask:

1. **Select** and **expand** the layer containing the mask in the Timeline panel. In our case, we select and expand the Car.mp4 layer.

On your screen, you'll see that the CTI is at the 10 seconds mark. We want to animate the morphing of an ellipse into a man. For this, we need to change the shape of the mask path into an ellipse using the Mask Path property.

2. **Click** the Time-Vary stop watch button for the <u>Mask Path</u> property. A new keyframe is added at the CTI, which is at 10 seconds mark.

3. **Move** the CTI to a new location. In our case, we move it to the first frame in the timeline by pressing the Home key.

4. Click the **Shape** underlined text for the <u>Mask Path</u> property. It opens the Mask Shape dialog box on the screen.

5. Select the **Reset To** check box in the <u>Shape</u> section. Then select the option: **Ellipse** from the <u>Reset To</u> dropdown list.

6. Click the **OK** button to close the dialog box. The mask path changes into an ellipse. You can see on your screen that a keyframe is added at the first frame.

7. Press the **Spacebar** key to preview the animation. You can see the shape of the mask path gradually changing from one shape to another in 10 seconds. Alternatively, you can add keyframes at different time marks on the timeline, and modify the mark path manually to animate into different shapes.

It's helpful to know that if you want the playhead to jump between keyframes on the timeline, you need to press the J and K keys on the keyboard. The J key makes the playhead jump to the previous keyframe; whereas, the K key makes the playhead jump to the next frame. You can also navigate from keyframe to keyframe using the Go to Next and Go to Previous arrows to the side of the property name display.

Lesson 16
Using Mask Feather Tool
Mask Feather Tool is one of the new additions in After Effects CS6. It allows you to add and refine feather around a mask by defining points along it. To modify mask feather, select Mask Feather Tool and then click the mask path. Now you can click and drag to control the mask feather. Mask Feather Tool is present as a hidden tool under Pen Tool on the Tools panel. Press the G key to toggle between Pen Tool and Mask Feather Tool by default. However, if you want to toggle between all the tools under Pen Tool by pressing G key, ensure that the Pen Tool Shortcut Toggles Between Pen and Mask Feather Tools check box is unchecked in the Preferences dialog box. Perform these steps to use Mask Feather Tool:

1. **Select** the mask path on the Composition panel of your After Effects screen. Then select **Mask Feather Tool** from the Tools panel.

2. **Click** the mask path on the Composition panel. Then **move** the Mask Feather Tool cursor over the mask path and **drag** it to add a feather. A plus sign appears with the Mask Feather Tool cursor. Similarly, you can add multiple control points by clicking and dragging on the mask path.

3. **Move** the Mask Feather Tool cursor over another location on the mask path and then **drag** the mask path to control the mask feather.

Working with Track Mattes

Mattes are layers that are used to define the transparent areas of a layer. Using track mattes, you can show one layer through a transparent area (hole) in another layer. In a track matte, white-color defines opaque areas, and black color defines transparent areas. While masks use vector-based paths to isolate areas of layer, track mattes use either alpha (transparency) or luminance (brightness). In most cases, alpha channels are used as track mattes. In cases, where the source image does not include an alpha channel, you can use a track matte other than the alpha channel. You can also animate a track matte by adding keyframes for the track matte layer's properties, such as scale, position, and vertices, or by animating the effects.

You need two layers to set up a track matte; one to act as a track matte and another to fill the hole in the track matte. You can animate either the track matte layer or the fill layer. It is important to place the track matte layer above the layer to be masked out. You can add one track matte per masked layer. In case you need multiple layers, you can combine those layers into a new composition; you can create pre-composition.

To create track mattes, you can also use graphic programs, such as Photoshop and Illustrator other than After Effects. Photoshop also has a timeline similar to After Effects for creating animation. After creating the animation in Photoshop, you can import the animated Photoshop file as a video file into After Effects. Perform the following steps to create a track matte using a type layer:

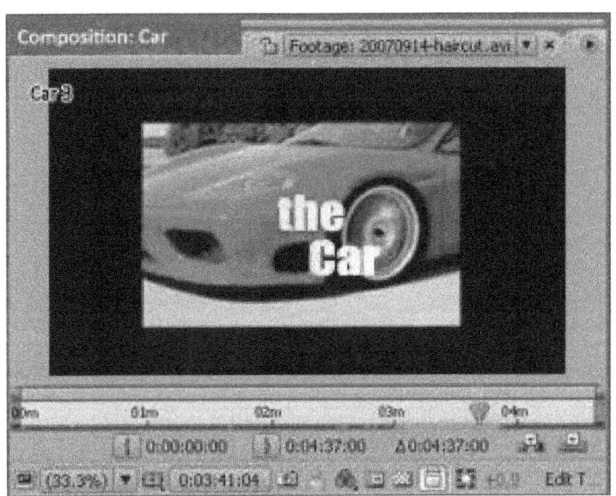

Picture 5.3

1. **Create** a composition and **import** the layer that you want to use into the Timeline panel. Then **select** Horizontal Type Tool from the Tools panel.

2. **Type** a text on the Composition panel. In our case, we have typed the Car, as shown in picture 5.3. You can **format** the text as required.

3. Click the **Choose grid and guide options** button at the bottom of the Composition panel and select the **Title/Action Safe** option. The title safe guides are displayed on the Composition panel; you can use them to safely place the title.

4. **Place** the title safely using the Selection Tool. Then click the **Choose grid and guide options** button at the bottom of the Composition panel and select the **Title/Action Safe** option again to hide the title safe guides.

5. Click the **Toggle Switches / Modes** button at the bottom of the Timeline panel to display the **TrkMat** column, which is hidden by default. You can use the TrkMat column to apply track mattes. The TrkMat column appears in the Timeline panel.

You can also how or hide columns by clicking the Expand or Collapse the Layer Switches pane, Expand or Collapse the Transfer Controls pane, or Expand or Collapse the In/Out/Duration/Stretch buttons at the lower-left corner of the Timeline panel.

6. In the Timeline panel, select the **Alpha Matte "the Car"** option from the <u>TrkMat column</u> pop-up menu for the Car.mp4 layer. The options in the pop-up menu are discussed as follows:

No Track Matte: Allows the layer above track matte layer to act as a normal layer with no transparency.
Alpha Matte: Creates opaque areas when alpha channel pixel value is 100%.
Alpha Inverted Matte: Creates opaque areas when alpha channel pixel value is 0%.
Luma Matte: Creates opaque areas when the luminance value of a pixel is 100%.
Luma Inverted Matte: Creates opaque areas when the luminance value of a pixel is 0%.

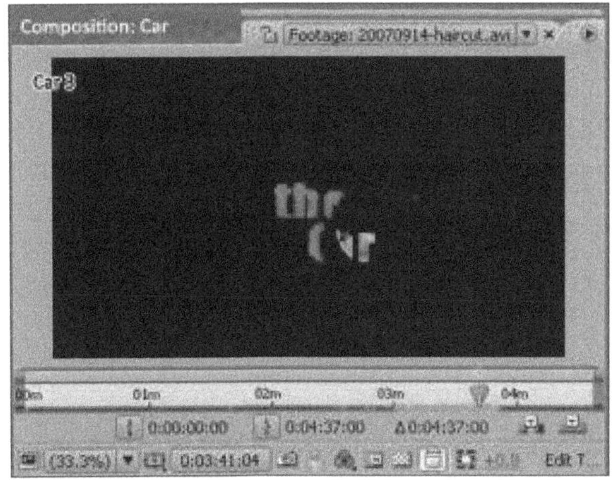

The text area now displays only the Car.mp4 layer, as shown in picture 5.4. Let us now create a pre-composition from the current composition.

7. **Select** both layers (the Car and Car.mp4) in the Timeline panel. Then choose **Layer> Pre-Compose** from the Menu bar to create a pre-composition. The Pre-compose dialog box will appear on your After Effects screen.

8. **Type** a name (the car) in the Name text box. Then click the **OK** button. The new pre-composition appears automatically.

Picture 5.4

9. **Place** the footage below the pre-composition in the Timeline panel. In our case, we have added the Car.mp4 layer. As the result in the Composition panel, the text (the Car) is not easily visible, by default. To differentiate the edge from the layer beneath, you can add an effect, such as drop shadow and hue/saturation.

Working with Chroma Key

Chroma keying is a technique that allows you to composite two layers together by removing a specific color from one layer to reveal the layer behind it. Mostly, you can use Chroma keying to separate a blue or green screen from a video and replace it with a different background. This technique is also referred to as color keying, blue screening, or green screening. However, you can also use solid colors, such as red and magenta for a background. In motion graphics, red screens are often used for shooting non-human objects, such as miniature models of cars and space ships; while magenta screens are used for creating visual effects. Chroma keying is often used on television in weather reporting and films where virtual backgrounds are used.

It is important to set up a blue screen or green screen with even lighting avoiding shadow, as it is a best practice to have the most narrow color range for Chroma keying. Shadows present itself as a darker color to the camera, which is difficult to register for replacement. A matte surface is preferred over a shiny surface, while working with Chroma keying. A matte surface diffuses the reflected light that facilitates a more even color range. In the subsequent sections, you learn about creating a garbage matte, creating a Chroma key, and refining the matte. Let's begin with learning to create a garbage mask.

Creating a Garbage Matte

When using a green or blue screen, the area around the subject is very important. However, while filming a video, you intentionally or unintentionally include extra elements in the video frame. The first step in the Chroma keying process is to create a garbage matte; this is a mask drawn to remove unnecessary areas of a video frame and to isolate the subject and the area immediately around it. While filming a blue or green screen shot, you often see parts of the set, such as light stand or the spot boys holding the light stand or frames. The garbage matte removes all those extra elements from the video frame and helps you to focus on the subject. The garbage matte has to completely enclose the subject.

Picture 5.5

If the subject is moving, you need to animate the vertices of the mask to accommodate the movement of the subject in the video frame. Picture 5.5 shows a video frame in the Footage panel with extra elements that you can mask out using a garbage matte. In this picture you can see a building appearing on the left of the video frame. To quickly hide the building, you can create a garbage mask using the shape tools, such as Rectangle Tool or Ellipse tool or Pen tool. Keep in mind that you need to create enough vertices when creating a garbage matte to be able to animate the mask to fit the movement of the subject. Perform these steps to create a garbage matte:

1. **Create** a new composition with the required footage. In our case, we have created a new composition called <u>Garbage Matte</u> and placed two footage items (Garbage Mask & Signature.mp4) in the Timeline panel.

2. **Select** the layer containing the green screen in the Timeline panel. In our case, we select the <u>Garbage Mask</u> layer.

Picture 5.6

3. **Move** the playhead (CTI) to a time mark (5 seconds) on the timeline, where the subject takes maximum area on the screen. Keep in mind that when subjects are moving in the green or blue screen footage, it is important to make sure the garbage matte is large enough to accommodate the subject's action.

4. **Select** the shape tool (Pen Tool) that you want to use to create the garbage mask. Then **draw** a garbage mask covering the area that you want to keep. The picture 5.6 shows the garbage mask drawn with the Pen Tool.

You will see on your screen that the garbage mask hides the building element of the frame displaying the underneath layer. It is always preferred to create a large garbage mask to not cut out any of the subject's movement. Alternatively, you can create a smaller mask that matches contours of the figure of the subject and then animate the position of the vertices on the path using the Mask Path property.

Creating a Chroma Key

Chroma keying is used to remove the green or blue screen from a video footage recorded for creating special effects. This technique is used to seamlessly combine live-action footage with the CG footage. For instance, you can shoot an actor against a green or blue background, remove the background using the Chroma keying technique, and then add the CG footage as the new background. There are various Chroma keys, namely: Color Key, Color Range, Difference Matte, Extract, Keylight (1.2), and Luma Key in After Effects, which can be used as required to remove the green screen.

In this case, you learn to use a very powerful Chroma key plug-in of After Effects, namely: Keylight (1.2). Similar to any other key effects, Keylight (1.2) creates transparent areas by keying out a specified range of colors on a single click. In addition, it has many options that you can use to fine tune the keying effect. You can use the key on backgrounds that consist of more than one color or on blue or green screens, which is unevenly lit and contains different shades of the same color. Perform the following steps to remove the green screen using Keylight (1.2):

1. **Select** the layer containing the green screen in the Timeline panel. In our case, we have selected the Garbage Mask layer created in the previous section.

2. Choose **Effect> Keying> Keylight (1.2)** from the Menu bar. It opens the Effect Controls panel with the properties for the Keylight (1.2) effect, if it is not already opened. The Keylight (1.2) effect includes various options such as Screen Color, Screen Gain, Screen Balance, Despill Bias, and alpha Bias.

3. **Click** the eyedropper which is on the right side of Screen Color option in the Effects Controls panel. Then **click** the color that you want to remove. In our case, we click the blue color which is in the background of the face already shown in picture 5.6.

This way, it keys out the blue color from the footage, as shown in picture 5.7. With one click, it removes the blue color. Now, let's fine tune the keying effect using other options in the Effect Controls panel. It is always best to use the Composition panel to precisely pick the color that you want to key out as you can see the color.

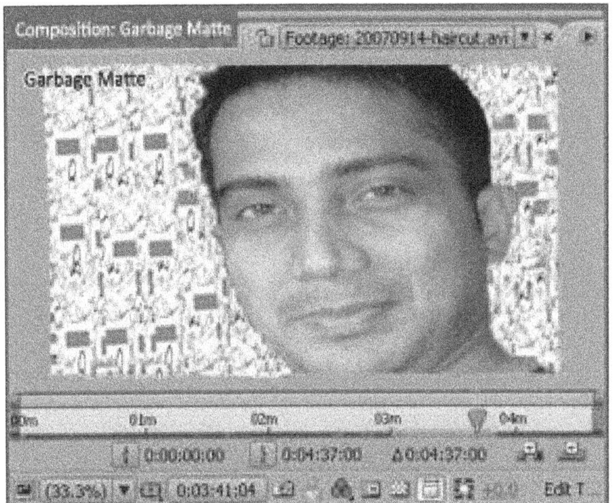

Picture 5.7

4. Select the **Status** option from the View dropdown list to view a grayscale preview of the effect. The Final Result is selected as the default view.

In the Status view, the white represents completely opaque areas, black represents completely transparent areas, and gray represents semi-transparent areas. Ideally, a good result can be achieved by removing semi-transparent areas, by removing gray color.

5. **Increase** the Screen Grain value to increase the black. In our case, we have set it as 150.0. Then **expand** the Screen Matte group to display more options.

6. **Set** the Clip Black value to 7.0. Then **set** the Clip White value to 90.0 to make white more opaque in the final result.

7. **Select** the Final Result option from the View dropdown list to view the final output after all modifications. Now it will show the effect of Keylight (1.2) on your screen.

You can see on your screen that the blue color is completely removed from the footage. However, if you still have trouble isolating the subject from the blue background using one key, you can try using a different one.

Refining a Matte

After the chroma key is created, it is often necessary to refine the mask that it creates to remove additional background area. The chroma key effect tends to leave a fringe around the subjects, which is visible when you zoom in on the Composition panel. To remove such fringe areas, you can use effects, such as Matte Choker. It is usually best to combine different effects, instead of trying to get the output from one effect.

The Matte Choker effect enables you to both choke (tighten) and spread (loosen) a matte, and removes the blue border. You can use this effect to fill in transparent holes that can be created as a result of using a keying effect or to modify the edge of a keyed area. Following are the three properties for the Matte Choker effect:

Geometric Softness: Specifies the largest possible spread or choke for the effect.
Choke: Sets the amount of the choke or spread. A positive value chokes a matte, while a negative value spreads a matte.
Gray Level Softness: Specifies the softness of the edges of the matte. Now you can perform the following steps to refine a matte using the Matte Choker effect:

1. **Select** a layer with the Keylight (1.2) effect in the Timeline panel. Then select the **400%** option in the Magnification ratio popup dropdown list at the bottom of the Composition panel to zoom in.

2. Choose **Effect> Matte> Matte Choker** from the Menu bar. It will show the result of the default settings on your screen.

The default settings of the effect usually remove the border; however, you can modify its settings in the Effect Controls panel to remove the blue or green border.

3. Set a **Geometric Softness 1** value in the Effect Control panel. In our case, we set it to 6.0. Then set a **Choke 1** value. In our case, we set it to 80. This removes and softens the matte edge for this footage.

4. Select the **Fit** option from the Magnification ratio popup dropdown list to zoom out the frame and fit the Composition panel. If you want, you can further add other effects, such as Color Correction effect to match the color theme of both layers.

Using Color Corrections

In the world of motion graphics, the terms color correction and color grading is often used interchangeably. Most footage imported into After Effects is shot in different conditions. Therefore, they require certain degree of color correction to make them consistent. Using color corrections, you can optimize the source footage to focus attention on a key element in a shot, correct errors in white balance and exposure, or ensure color consistency from one shot to another. After Effects includes several built-in effects for color correction, such as Curves, Levels, Black & White, Color Balance, and other effects in the Color Correction effect category.

To select a color correction effect, select Effect> Color Correction from the Menu bar and then select any effect from the list. You can also apply multiple color correction effects on a single layer. All the effects and their properties appear in the Effect Controls panel, which appears automatically when you apply an effect on a layer. When you assemble a composition, you may want to adjust or correct the colors of one or more layers of the any of the following reasons:

- To make multiple footage items merge seamlessly, as though shot under the same conditions and composite the footage items together.
- To adjust the colors of a day shot to make it appear as if shot at night.
- To adjust, the exposure of an image to recover details in case of over-exposed highlights.
- To increase, one color of a video when you need to composite a graphic element, such as a logo over the video.
- To limit colors to a particular range of colors, such as the broadcast-safe range.

After knowing about the reasons of color correction, now you can perform the following steps on your computer to color correct in After Effects CS6:

1. **Select** the layer that you want to color correct in the Timeline panel. In our case, we select the Car.mp4 layer.

2. Choose **Effect> Color Correction> Hue/Saturation** from the Menu bar. It opens the Effect Controls panel on the screen.

The Effect Controls panel appears with options for the selected color correct effect. By default, the Master option is selected in the Channel Control dropdown list, which modifies all the colors simultaneously.

3. Set the **Master Hue** option as: 0x +156.0^0. You can notice the change on the Composition panel of your screen.

4. Set the **Master Saturation** option as: 13. Then set the **Master Lightness** option as -3. The result of the Hue/Saturation effect appears on the Composition panel.

Similarly, to modify the values for individual colors, such as Reds, Yellows, and Cyans, select it from the Channel Control dropdown list. After Effects provides various built-in color correction effects that you can use to create different effects. In addition, you can also use third-party effects. With this, we come to the end of the chapter.

Lesson 17
Working with Effects, Presets, and Audio
In After Effects, similar to filters in Photoshop, effects are used to apply special effects, such as glow, blur, noise, or color correction to a layer. To create fascinating motion graphics, you must be comfortable working with the wide range of built-in effects available in After Effects and third-party plug-ins. In addition, there are a number of animation presets that you can use to create motion graphics. Animation presets are essentially pre-built rendered animations. They can be single or combination of effects. You can apply effects and animation presets to a layer to change its appearance non-destructively. By default, the duration of effects and animation presets matches to the duration of the layer. However, you can start and stop the effect as required. You can also save combinations of layer properties, animations, and effects as an animation preset and reuse them on other layers.

Using the Effects & Presets panel, you can locate all the effects and animation presets to apply them on a selected layer. To apply an effect, double-click on it in the Effects & Presets panel. You can also use the Bridge application to apply the effects and animation presets. To add realism to motion graphics, you can also add audio and synchronize it with an animation. For instance, while creating a bomb blast effect, you can add an audio containing the sound generated during a real world bomb blast. You can import an audio into the composition similar to any other footage items. You can also add audio effects, such as Delay, Reverb, and Backwards to the audio. In this chapter, you first learn about the Effects & Presets and Effect Controls panels. Next, you learn to select and apply effects on a layer and a mask. You also learn to animate an effect. In addition, you learn to select and apply animation presets, and save a custom animation presets. Towards the end, you learn to add, trim, and loop an audio, and apply audio effects on it.

Exploring the Effects & Presets Panel
The Effects & Presets panel lists all built-in effects and animation presets in After Effects. Using this panel, you can browse for an effect or animations preset and apply it on a layer. By default, the Effects and Presets panel is visible in the default After Effects workspace (Standard). In case the panel is not visible, you can open it by selecting Window> Effects and Presets from the Menu bar or by pressing the Ctrl+S keys together. You can also use the Effects workspace while working with effects and animation presets. This workspace includes panels, such as Effects and Presets and Effect Controls that are essential to work with effects and animation presets.

Alternatively, you can access effects and animation presets using the Menu bar. Using the Effect menu, you can apply an effect to the selected layers. When you open the Effects & Presets panel on your screen, it will come up showing effects and animation presets categories. In this panel, to browse for an effect or animation preset, scroll through the list of effects and animation presets by expanding the respective categories. You can also search for them by typing a part of the name in the search field, shown in picture 5.8 with the red arrow numbered 1. As you start typing, After Effects automatically searches for the effect or animation preset and displays a list of effects resembling the text in the panel. For instance, when you type the word drop in the search field, the Effects & Presets panel shows the result including Drop Bounce, Eyedropper Fill, and Drop Shadow. When you enter a name in the search field, the close (x) button appears to the right of the search field. To clear the search field, you can click the close button. Keep in mind that the Project, Timeline, and Effects & Presets panels each contain search fields that you can use to filter items in the panel. You can also control how the Effects & Presets panel displays the list of effects and animation presets.

Teach Yourself Adobe After Effects | Niranjan Jha Showman | Cromosys Publication

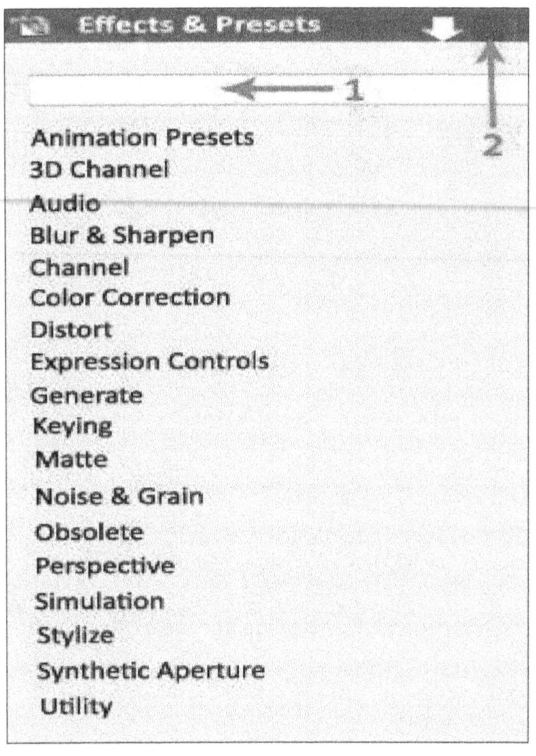

Picture 5.8

If you click a small **rectangular button** at the top-right of the Effects & Presets panel (shown in picture 5.8 with the red arrow numbered 2), it opens the Effects & Presets panel menu. Using this panel menu, you can access several options, such as Undock Panel, Close Panel, Save Animation Preset, and Browse Presets. This panel organizes effects and animation presets based on the options, such as Categories, Explorer Folders, or Alphabetical, which you select from the Effects & Presets panel menu. The option that you select determines the items to be displayed. By default, the Categories view is selected. You can also select the Explorer Folders or Alphabetical view. In the Alphabetical view, the Effects & Presets panel lists individual effects and animation presets alphabetically. Other options in the Effects & Presets panel menu are discussed as follows:

- Show Effects for All Color Depths: Shows effects that are compatible with any color depth of images, instead of the current project. By default, this option is selected.

- Show Effects: Shows all built-in as well as third party effects in After Effects. By default, this option is selected.
- Show Animation Presets: Shows all animation presets, including custom animation presets that you have saved in the Presets folder. By default, this option is selected.
- Reveal in Explorer: Opens the folder that contains the effect or animation preset selected in the Effects & Presets panel. By default, this option is not selected.
- Refresh List: Updates the list of effects and animation presets. By default, this option is not selected.

Exploring the Effects Controls Panel

The Effect Controls panel allows you to work with effects and their controls (properties). You can customize an effect by modifying its properties as required in the Effect Controls panel. By default, the Effect Controls panel is hidden when the Standard workspace is selected. To display the panel in the Standard workspace, you need to select Window> Effect Controls from the Menu bar. With a layer selected in the Timeline panel, press the F3 key to toggle the Effect Controls panel visibility. However, when you apply an effect to a layer, the Effect Controls panel opens automatically with controls to modify the applied effect. You can also select the Effect workspace to display the Effect Controls panel, which by default appears grouped with the Project panel. You can go ahead and open the Effect Controls panel to see it on the screen.

When you look at the Effect Controls panel, you will find two effects (Drop Shadow and Hue/Saturation) and their controls. This panel allows you to apply multiple effects to a layer. The effects applied first appear at the top of the stacking order in the Effect Controls panel. The most recent effect applied or modified appears selected. You can expand or collapse an effect by clicking the dropdown arrow on the left of their respective name. When you apply an effect, it appears in the expanded mode by default. You can also expand or collapse the active effect by pressing the Right Arrow and Left Arrow keys, respectively. In addition, press the Down Arrow key to select the next effect in the stacking order, or the Up Arrow key to select the previous effect. To delete an effect, select it and the press the Delete key.

In the Effect Controls panel tab, there is an Effect Controls Viewer that allows you to choose the layer for which the controls are displayed in the panel. You can access the Effect Controls Viewer by clicking the **down arrow button** (˅) which is at the top and beside (right side) the title tag: Effect Controls. The Effect Controls Viewer is useful for multiple layers in the composition with effects. By the way, you can also work with effects and change most of the effect controls in the Timeline panel. However, in the Effect Controls panel, there are controls, such as sliders, effect control point buttons, and histograms that allow you to customize the effect interactively.

Applying Effects

To apply an effect on a layer, first locate the effect in the Effect & Presets panel, and then drag and drop the effect from the Effect & Presets panel onto the layer in the Timeline or the Composition panel. You can also double-click an effect in the Effect & Presets panel to apply it on a selected layer. You can also apply an effect using the Menu bar. When you drag an effect onto a layer in the Composition panel, the Info panel displays the name of the layer under the mouse pointer. You can also apply an effect on multiple layers simultaneously by selecting those layers. You can also copy an effect from a layer and apply it to one or more layers; for this, use the Copy command under the Edit menu to copy the effect, and then use the Paste command to paste it on the target layer. Note that if no layer is selected or the mouse-pointer is not hovering over a layer, on releasing the mouse button or double-clicking an effect, nothing changes.

Locating Effects in the Effects & Presets Panel

The Effect & Presets panel serves as a library of effects in After Effects. It lists all effects and animation presets. To locate an effect in the Effect & Presets panel, you can browse through categories or use the search field. Using the search feature of the Effect & Presets panel, you can easily access the effects, which makes the Effect & Presets panel the preferred choice for selecting and applying effects. You can also select and apply an effect using the Effect menu. In this section, you learn to locate an effect using the Effect & Presets panel. Perform the following steps to locate an effect in the Effect & Presets panel:

1. **Click** the search field in the Effect & Presets panel to activate it. Alternatively, you can click the Effect & Presets panel to make it the active panel, and then press the Ctrl+F keys to activate the search field.

2. **Type** the initial few letters of the effect name in the search field. In our case, we type: shar, which is the initial of the Sharpen effects.

As you type the letters in the search field, the effects and animation presets that match the typed letters are displayed in the Effect & Presets panel. As you can see in the figure, two effects with 'shar' as part of their name appear. In our case, the Sharpen and Unsharp Mask effects appear under the Blur & Sharpen effects group. You can also see that the icons which represent the effects slightly different from the icons which represent the animation presets.

3. **Click** an effect (Sharpen effect) to select. While typing in the search field, you would have noticed that options appear allowing you to save the search item.

To start a new search, you need to clear the search field using the Backspace key or click the close icon in the search field. Alternatively, if you know the folder that contains the effect, you can select it using the Effect menu; for instance, choose Effect> Blur & Sharpen> Sharpen from the Menu bar to select the Sharpen effect.

Applying an Effect on a Layer

To apply an effect, select a layer on which you want to apply it, browse for the effect, and then drag it on the layer in the Timeline or Composition panel. You can also double-click the effect to apply it on the selected layer. In After Effects, there are effects that you can apply to different types of layers, such as solid, text, shape, or video layer. After Effects treats solid layers as any other footage item. There are effects that can be applied only to solid layers; for instance, you can apply the Radio Waves effect only to a solid layer. In this section, you learn to apply the CC Tiler effect. Perform the following steps to apply the CC Tiler effect to a layer:

1. **Select** the layer in the Timeline panel. In our case, we select Car.mp4 layer, (picture 5.9). Then click the **search** filed in the <u>Effects & Presets</u> panel and type **tiler** in it. After Effects filters and shows the CC Tiler effect.

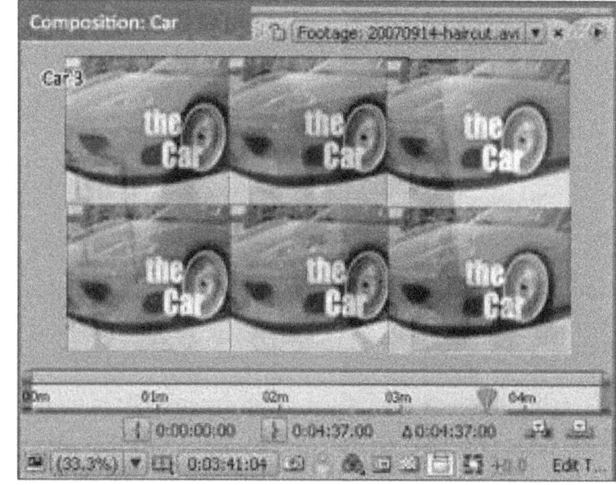

Picture 5.9   Picture 6.0

2. **Click** and **drag** the CC Tiler effect from the Effects & Presets panel and **drop** it on the layer in the Timeline panel. Alternatively, you can select Effect> Distort> CC Tiler from the Menu bar.

It is important to know that if you drag an effect over the Composition panel, it applies to the top-most layer. However, if a layer is locked, the effect is applied on the layer beneath it. The Effect Controls panel appears with controls for the CC Tiler effect. The controls for the CC Tiler effect include Scale, Center, and Blend w. Original. You can modify these controls to change the effect. By default, Scale control is set to 100.0%.

3. **Set** the <u>Scale control</u> to any value. In our case, we set it to 40.0%. It creates the CC Tiler effect as shown in picture 6.0.

The CC Tiler effect creates nine tiles in the Composition panel. Reducing the scale value increases the number of tiles. The Center control allows you to move the tiles. The Blend w. Original control blends the tiler effect with the original layer. Picture 6.0 shows the CC Tiler effect with the Blend w. Original control value set to 50.0%.

Applying Effects on a Mask

In After Effects, you can apply various effects on a mask. Masks help you to hide or reveal parts of a layer. You can create masks using the shape tools or Pen Tool in After Effects or import them from vector-based drawing programs, such as Illustrator. To apply an effect to a mask, select the layer with the mask, and then select the effect that you want to apply using the steps explained in the previous section. Thus, you can add special effects to a portion of a layer. For instance, you can add the Hue/Saturation effect to a mask to colorize a portion of a layer. Perform the following steps to apply an effect on a mask:

1. **Open** a composition with a layer containing a mask in the Timeline panel. In our case, we open the Mask 2 composition.

2. **Type** hue in the search field to show the Hue/Saturation effect. Alternatively, choose Effect> Color Correction> Hue/Saturation from the Menu bar.

3. **Drag** the Hue/Saturation effect on the mask layer (Car.mp4) in the Timeline panel. The Hue/Saturation effect controls appear on the Effect Controls panel.

The default settings have no effects on the layer. To customize the effect, modify the controls as required. In our case, we modify the Master Hue and Master Saturation controls.

4. Set the **Master Hue** value to 0x +125.0. Then set the **Master Saturation** value to 50. The Hue/Saturation effect appears on the mask layer of your screen.

Animating Effects

After Effects is primarily dependent on manipulating various effect controls, instead of using tools to create new effects from scratch. It provides a number of built-in effects that you can animate similar to a layer. Using controls in the Effect Controls or Timeline panel, you can animate an effect. Controls with a stop watch indicate that you can animate them. You can also use the Timeline panel to animate on effect.

The basic workflow of animating an effect is to move the Current Time Indicator (CTI or playhead) to any time period, activate the Time-Vary stop watch for the control that you want to animate. Now, change the value, move the playhead to another time period, and change the value again. That's it. The effects in the Generate group are animated by default; however, you can modify an animation by changing the values. For instance, you can animate the Mosaic effect to create animated backgrounds in After Effects. When you animate an effect, there might be long delays, as the After Effects application builds a preview. This is due to the speed of the computer and the power of needed to build and preview certain effects. Perform the following steps on your computer to create an animated background using the Mosaic effect:

1. **Select** a layer (Mask.mp4) in the Timeline panel. Then **type**: mosai in the search field of the Effects & Presets panel.

2. **Drag** the Mosaic effect onto the Composition panel and **drop** to apply. You can also double-click an effect on the Effects & Presets panel to apply it on a selected layer.

The Effects Control panel appears with the controls for the Mosaic effect shown on the Composition. You can see on your screen that the default values for Horizontal Blocks and Vertical Blocks controls are both set to 10. You can animate these controls to animate the mosaic effect. In our case, the playhead is at the start of the timeline, which is 0:00:00:00.

3. **Click** the Time-Vary stop watches for both Horizontal Blocks and Vertical Blocks controls to enable animation.

4. **Move** the playhead to any time frame in the Timeline panel. In our case, we move the playhead to 0:00:02:21 mark.

5. In the Project panel (on the left of Composition panel), you can see the **Reset** option next to the Mosaic tag. So under the Reset option, **change** the values for the Horizontal Blocks and Vertical Blocks controls to 20 each.

This adds more blocks on the layer. As the Time-Vary stop watches are enabled, the animation is created, which can be previewed.

6. Press the **Home** key to move the playhead to the start of the timeline, and then press the **Spacebar** key to preview the animation.

Selecting and Applying Animation Presets

After Effects provides hundreds of animation presets that you can apply to layers and modify as required. Animation presets are great source for quickly creating an animated background and predefined animations. Many animation presets do not contain animation; rather, they contain combinations of effects and transform properties. You can apply animation presets to text, solid, and shape layers. You can select an animation preset from the Effects & Presets panel, the Effect menu, and the Bridge application. There is an advantage of the Bridge application over the Effects & Presets panel; you can preview an animation before applying it. You can also save animation presets and transfer them from one computer to the other. The filename extension used for an animation preset is .ffx. The animation presets that are installed with After Effects are in the Presets folder. In this section, you learn to apply an animation preset using the Effects & Presets panel. Perform the following steps to select and apply an animation preset on a layer:

1. **Select** a layer on which you want to apply an animation preset. In our case, we select the Mask.mp4 layer.

2. **Expand** the Animation Presets group in the Effects & Presets panel. Then expand the **Image – Special Effects** group.

3. Double-click the **Bad TV 2 – old** animation preset. The Bad TV 2 – old animation preset is applied on the selected layer. Then **preview** the video layer to see the old TV effects on the Mask.mp4 layer.

You can see on your screen that the selected animation preset creates an old TV effect. The Effect Controls panel appears with the controls for the selected animation preset. The Bad TV 2 – old animation preset is the combination of various effects including Wave Warp, Box Blur, Color Balance (HLS), Noise, and Venetian Blinds. You can further modify the controls in the effects to modify the animation preset as required. Keep in mind that unlike using the Effects & Presets panel, when you apply an animation preset using the Bridge, the Effect Controls panel does not appear.

Saving an Animation Preset

Animation presets are fully editable in After Effects. It means you can customize them to satisfy the needs. You can also create custom animation presets that can contain animated effects. In addition to the effects and their properties, the animation preset also includes keyframes and expressions. For instance, if you create smoke using several effects with complex property settings and keyframes, you can save all these settings as a single animation preset. You can then apply this animation preset to any other layer.

It is important to know the position of the playhead before applying and saving animation presets. Any keyframes that are saved with the animation preset are added to the timeline; the first keyframe in the preset is placed at the current position of the playhead, and the rest are placed relative to the first keyframe to maintain the timing of the overall animation. Perform the following steps to save an animation preset:

1. **Select** a composition with the customized animation that you want to save as a preset. In our case, we select the Bad TV composition.

2. **Select** a layer (Mask.mp4) in the Timeline panel and press the **U key** to display only the animated properties.

3. **Move** the playhead to the beginning (0:00:00:00) of the timeline. Then **select** all effects in the Effect Controls panel. To select all (multiple) effects, hold the Shift key down and click the effects that you want to select.

4. Choose **Animation> Save Animation Preset** from the Menu bar. It opens the Save Animation Preset dialog box.

5. **Select** a location to save the preset from the <u>Save in</u> dropdown list. In our case, we select the default **Image – Special Effects** folder.

6. **Type** a new name for the preset in the File name combo box. In our case, we type **Bad TV Modified**. Then click the **Save** button to save the animation preset.

You can now select and apply this custom animation preset in any other project by typing its name in the search field of the Effects & Presets panel. In case this animation preset does not appear in the Effects & Preset panel, select the Refresh List option from the Effects & Presets panel menu.

Lesson 18
Working with Audio

Audio is one of the media types used in After Effects animations. You can import and add the audio into the composition similar to other media types. In the Timeline panel, the audio appears in a separate layer called as an audio layer. The audio layer includes the **Audio layer switch** (a speaker icon), which allows you to mute or unmute an audio. To preview an audio, you must ensure that the Audio layer switch is enabled. The Audio layer switch also appears for those video layers with audio included in it.

When you preview an audio, the animated audio levels are displayed in the Audio panel. To display the Audio panel, select Window> Audio from the Menu bar; it is not displayed by default. In After Effects, you can preview an audio in the following three ways:

- Press the Period key on the keyboard to preview the audio in a composition. This begins playing the audio in real-time.
- Use the RAM preview function by pressing the Zero key on the keyboard to preview the audio.
- Drag the playhead forward or backward in the time ruler while holding the Ctrl key down on the keyboard to preview the audio file.

In After Effects, there are several audio effects that you can apply on an audio layer to create interesting audio effects. For instance, you can create a fading out audio using the Stereo Mixer effect, because it uses an amplitude percentage rather than a decibel (db) value. You can import any of the following types of audio files into After Effects: Adobe Sound Document (ASND), Advanced Audio Coding (AAC), Audio Interchange File Format (AIF, AIFF), MP3 (MP3, MPEG, MPG), Video for Windows (AVI, WAV), Waveform (WAV). It is important to know that in motion graphics, the frame rate plays an important role as it varies depending on the output format of the composition. In addition, it is useful in synchronizing audio with an animation.

Adding Audio

Similar to any other media type, audio files are imported into the Project panel. Similar to any footage item, you can add audio files to a composition by dragging and dropping the files from the Project panel to the Timeline panel. Unlike a still image and video footage item, audio is not visible in the Composition panel. However, you ca show the waveform display of the audio in the Timeline panel using the Waveform property in the Audio property group. Unlike other layers, audio layers do not include the Transform property group; instead, they include only the Audio Level property, which allows you to control the volume of the audio file.

Using the Import command, you can import audio into the project. The Import command places the audio file into the highlighted folder in the Project panel. If there are no folders in the Project panel or no folders are highlighted, the audio file is placed onto the main Project panel. Perform the following steps to add an audio file to a composition:

1. **Create** a new or open an existing After Effects project in which you want to add an audio file. In our case, we select the Car 3 composition in the Timeline panel.

2. Import the audio file if already not imported using the **File> Import> File** option from the Menu bar. In our case, we have already imported the Car BG Music.mp3 audio file.

3. **Drag** the audio file from the Project panel over the Timeline panel. In our case, we drag the Car BG Music.mp3 audio file.

4. **Drop** the audio file below the layer in the Timeline panel. In our case, we drop the audio file below the Car.mp4 layer. As the result, the audio file is added to the Car 3 composition in the Timeline panel and it appears below the Car.mp4 layer.

Trimming an Audio

The process of shortening an audio is known as trimming in After Effects. A little extra padding is often included at the beginning and end of an audio, which is known as handles. In case you want to remove this extra padding or use a small portion of a long audio, you need to shorten the audio. Trimming process hides the extra portion instead of deleting it.

Trimming at the beginning or end of an audio determines those frames of the audio to be first or last in the composition. You can trim an audio by changing the In Point and Out Point in the Layer panel or the Timeline panel. By default, the beginning of an audio is called the In Point, while the end of an audio is called the Out Point. Unlike still image layers, when you add an audio onto the Timeline panel, the audio layer appears with the original duration, irrespective of the composition duration. You can later adjust (trim) the In and Out Points manually to match the duration of an audio to the duration of the composition. To set the In Point manually, you can place Selection Tool at the beginning of an audio layer duration bar. A double-headed arrow appears; using this, you can click and drag the layer In Point to a different duration. Similarly, to set the Out Point manually, you can place Selection Tool at the end of an audio layer duration bar. A double-headed arrow appears; using this you can click and drag the layer Out Point to a different duration. Alternatively, you can press the Alt+[(left bracket) keys together to set the In Point of the layer at the current playhead position. Similarly, you can press the Alt+] keys to set the Out Point. Perform the following steps to trim an audio using the Layer panel:

1. **Select** an audio layer in the Timeline panel of the After Effects screen. In our case, we select the Car BG Music.mp3 layer. Then **double-click** the selected layer to open it in the Layer panel. The Layer panel is at the bottom of the Composition panel (already shown and explained in picture 2.5).

Alternatively, you can select Layer> Open Layer from the Menu bar to open the selected layer in the Layer panel. The Car BG Music.mp3 audio layer opens in the Layer panel. The Layer panel displays the layer before any transforms are applied to it. For instance, the Layer panel does not show the result of modifying the Scale property of a layer. The time ruler for the audio layer appears at the <u>bottom</u> of the **Layer panel**. By default, the playhead is placed at the start of the audio file.

2. Click the **Current Time** button (0:00:00:00) at the bottom of the <u>Layer panel</u> to change the current time indicated by the playhead position. It opens the <u>Go to Time</u> dialog box.

3. **Type**: 500 in the time text box of the Go to Time dialog box. The number is automatically converted to its time code equivalent, and displayed adjacent to the text box (500 is 0:00:05:00). Then click the **OK** button to go to the 5 seconds mark on the time ruler in the Layer panel as well as in the Timeline panel.

4. Click the **Set IN point to current time** button (<) in the Layer panel. This sets the In Point of the layer to the current time. In the Timeline panel, the playhead moves to the start.

5. Click the **Current Time** button (0:00:05:00) at the bottom of the Layer panel again. Then **type**: 1500 in the time text box of the Go to Time dialog box. The number is automatically converted to its time code equivalent and displayed adjacent to the text box (1500 is 0:00:15:00).

6. Click the **OK** button to go to the 15 seconds mark on the time ruler. Then click the **Set OUT point to current time** button (>) in the Layer panel.

This sets the Out Point of the layer to the current time, which is 15 seconds. In the Timeline and Layer panels, the audio layer appears for 10 seconds (from 5 to 15 seconds). If you click and drag the playhead through the time ruler, the playhead moves back and forward through the video file. You can use the technique called scrubbing the playhead, to navigate quickly to a specific time in the file. This is not a real-time preview; the speed at which you scrub the playhead controls the playback speed.

Using the Time Remapping Feature

In most cases, the duration of an audio is not as long as the composition; hence, you need to loop it to be able to play through the composition. By default, all the imported audio and video files are set to loop only once. However, you can loop the audio file using the time remapping feature of After Effects. Time remapping is a process that allows you to expand, compress, play backward, or freeze a portion of the duration of an audio file. For instance, you can play the audio forward, play the audio backward for few frames or seconds to make the audio retreat, and then play it forward again. When you enable the time remapping feature for an audio layer, a Time Remap keyframe is added at the start and end points of the layer. You can also change the loop settings in the Interpret Footage dialog box, which allows you to set various footage attributes, such as pixel aspect ratio, alpha channel type, frame rate, and color profile, manually.

When you import an audio file, you can check the file properties, such as time duration and number of times the file is used, above the Project panel. If you can see above the Project panel of your screen, you will find the duration of the audio file reads 0:01:03:01. In case the duration of the audio file is less than the current composition, you can use the time remapping feature to loop the audio. Perform the following steps to loop an audio clip using the time remapping feature:

1. **Select** an audio layer in the Timeline panel that you want to play in a loop. In our case, we select the Car Music.wav layer.

2. Choose **Layer> Time> Enable Time Remapping** from Menu bar. The Time Remap property appears for audio layer in the Timeline panel, and two Time Remap keyframes appear for the layer in the time ruler.

3. Click the **Time-Vary stop watch** button while pressing the Alt key for the Time Remap property of the audio layer. This sets the default expression for time remapping. It will show no immediate effect in the Composition panel.

4. Click the **Expression language** menu button (▶) for the **Expression: Time Remap** property of the audio layer. It opens a dropdown list.

5. **Choose** Property> loopOut(type ="cycle", numKeyframes = 0) from the dropdown list. The audio is now set to loop in a cycle, which plays the clip endlessly.

However, you need to extend the Out Point of the layer to the end of the composition. You can also see that the selected expression appears in the time ruler. By the way, an expression is a script that evaluates to a single value for a single layer property at a specific point-in-time.

6. **Click** the Car Music.wav layer in the Timeline panel to select it. Then press the **End key** to move the playhead to the end of the time ruler.

7. **Press** the Alt+] (right bracket) keys together to extend the layer to the end of the composition. You can also manually drag the end of the layer to extend the layer to the end of the composition.

8. Click the **Play/Pause** button in the <u>Preview</u> panel to watch the RAM preview of the entire composition. You can see that the audio clip plays repeatedly to the end of the composition.

Applying Audio Effects

After Effects is a popular choice for digital post-production of films and motion graphics. You can composite different audio layers and apply audio effects on them you can also apply audio effects to existing audio footage or synthesize any audio by combining the Tone effect with other audio effects. After Effects includes audio effects, such as Backwards, Bass & Treble, Delay, Modulator, Reverb, Stereo Mixer, and Tone. For instance, you can reverse the audio of a layer by playing the audio from the last frame to the first frame using the Backwards audio effect. You can select and apply an audio effect using the Effects & Presets panel or the Effect menu. You can display an audio waveform by selecting an audio layer in the Timeline panel and pressing the L key twice. Perform the following steps to add an audio effect on an audio layer:

1. **Select** an audio layer in the Timeline panel on which you want to apply an audio effect. In our case, we select the **Car BG Music.mp3** audio layer.

2. **Click** the dropdown arrow to the left of the <u>Audio</u> folder in the Effects & Presets panel to display the list of audio effects. By default, the following ten audio effects are included in After Effects:

- Backwards: Reverses an audio of a layer by playing it from the last frame to the first frame. When you apply this effect, the frames remain in their original order in the Timeline panel.
- Bass & Treble: Increases or decreases the low frequencies (bass) or the high frequencies (treble) of an audio.
- Delay: Repeats the audio after a specified amount of time.
- Flange & Chorus: Creates an audio effect by mixing the original audio with the copy of the original audio. The copied audio is delayed by a varying amount that cycle over time. The default settings for the Flange & Chorus effect are for flange.
- High-Low Pass: Sets a limit for audio frequencies to pass. High Pass allows frequencies above the limit and blocks frequencies below the limit; whereas, Low Pass allows frequencies below the limit and blocks frequencies above the limit.
- Modulator: Adds both vibrato and tremolo effects to audio by varying (modulating) the frequencies and amplitude. Vibrato is a musical effect consisting of a regular pulsating change of pitch, while tremolo describes various trembling effects.
- Parametric EQ: Emphasizes for attenuates specific frequency ranges. Parametric EQ is useful for enhancing music, such as boosting low frequencies to bring up bass.

- Reverb: Simulates a spacious or acoustically live interior by simulating random reflections of a sound off a surface.
- Stereo Mixer: Mixes the left and right channels of an audio and spreads the entire signal from one channel to another.
- Tone: Synthesizes simple audio tones to create sounds, such as the low rumble of a submarine, a telephone ringing in the background, sirens, or a laser blast.

3. **Select** an audio effect (Reverb) from the list. Then **drag** the Reverb audio effect and **drop** on the selected audio layer in the Timeline panel.

The Reverb effect is applied on the selected Car BG Music.mp3 layer and the Effect Controls panel appears with properties for the effect. To customize the audio effect, you can modify the controls. In our case, we have modified the Reverb Time (ms) control.

4. **Set** a new value for Reverb Time (ms). In our case, we set the value to 150.00. The default Reverb Time value is 100.00.

5. **Press** the Period key (.) to preview the audio only. With this section, we come to the end of the chapter.

Lesson 19
Rendering and Exporting
Rendering refers to combining all layers, layer effects, and other elements to create composite images. It is the final stage and usually the most time consuming in the workflow. To create a video, sequence of images or frames are rendered. Mostly, to see the preview of an effect, you may want to render a composition. In such case, you can crop (reducing frame size) or trim (reducing duration) a composition and render the specific frames that are involved in the current effect. You can define render settings depending on the output medium, such as computer, television, Web and mobile devices. Output Module allows you to encode the frames of the rendered composition into one or more output files. After Effects provides a range of video formats, such as Audio Video Interleave (AVI), Flash Video (FLV), and Moving Picture Expert Groups 4 (MPEG4), and codecs such as Xvid for the output. Codecs are mathematical algorithms that are used to compress audio and video files for lower file sizes. Exporting is useful when you want to use the After Effects projects in other software, such as Premiere Pro and Flash Professional. The format you choose to export depends on the medium to play the final output. If you use Adobe Premiere Pro to edit a video, you can use Adobe Dynamic Link to import un-rendered composition directly to the Premiere Pro timeline instead of rendering the composition in After Effects. In this lesson, you first learn to use the Render Queue panel. Next, you learn to render a composition, adjust render settings and duplicate a render item. In addition, you learn to trim and crop a composition. Towards the end, you learn to export a composition for the Web and mobile devices.

Understanding the Render Queue Panel
After creating motion graphics, you can render them using the Render Queue panel for the final output. The Render Queue panel provides an interface for rendering and exporting compositions. To render a composition, you need to place it in the Render Queue panel. When you place a composition into the Render Queue panel, the composition is called render item. You can add multiple render items to the

Render Queue panel to be rendered in a batch. The Render button located at the upper-right corner of the Render Queue panel allows you to render all the render items with the status of Queued. The render items are rendered in the order of their listing in the panel. When rendering is completed, the render status changes to Done. However, the render item remains in the Render Queue panel until it is removed manually. Note that you cannot re-render a rendered item; however, you can duplicate it to create a new render item in the queue with the same or new settings. By default, the Render Queue panel is not visible in the After Effects interface. To display the Render Queue panel, select Window> Render Queue from the Menu bar or press Alt+Ctrl+0 keys together. You can open the Render Queue panel on your screen. By the way, the Render Queue panel automatically opens when you add a composition to the render queue using the Add to Render Queue command from Composition panel.

The Render Queue panel includes the following two sets of options to configure:
Render Settings: Sets characteristics such as resolution, frame rate, and duration for an output file.
Output Module: Specifies settings for output format and compression. It also allows you to select a folder location and name for the output file using the Output To option.

When you add a composition into the Render Queue panel, it is queued in the panel and a number is provided to it in the stacking order. A progress bar appears at the top of the Render Queue panel, indicating the percentage of the rendered item. During rendering, the Stop and Pause buttons become active. You can also see on your screen that the status bar (at the bottom) of the Render Queue panel displays messages about the current rendering operation, such as Random Access Memory (RAM) being used in percentage, the render start time (Renders Started), Total Time Elapsed, and Most Recent Error. The Render button is enabled when you add a composition into the Render Queue panel. While rendering an item, the stop or pause buttons become active; hence, you can stop or pause the rendering as required. But while rendering is paused, you cannot change the settings or use any other options in the After Effects application. The status for each render item is displayed in the Status column of the Render Queue panel. Different types of status are discussed as follows:

Needs Output: Indicates that the output location for the render item is not specified
Rendering: Indicates that the rendering is in progress
Un-queued: Indicates that the render item is listed in the Render Queue panel, but not ready to render
Queued: Indicates that the render item is ready to render
Failed: Indicates that rendering the render item was unsuccessful
User Stopped: Indicates that the rendering process is stopped
Done: Indicates that the rendering process for the item is complete

Rendering a Composition

To render a composition with all the animations, effects, and masks, first you need to add it to the render queue. To add a composition to the render queue, you need to select Composition> Add to Render Queue from the Menu bar. You can render a single composition or multiple compositions by adding them to the render queue in the Render Queue panel. When you press the Render button, After Effects renders all the render items sequentially. Perform the following steps to render a composition:

1. **Double-click** a composition in the Project panel to make it active. In our case, we double-click Car 3 composition in the Project panel. A composition needs to be active in the Project or Composition panel to enable the Add to Render Queue command in the Composition menu.

2. Select **Composition> Add to Render Queue** from the Menu bar to add the selected composition as a render item. Alternatively, you can press the Ctrl+Shift+/ (forward slash) keys or Ctrl+M keys together to add the selected composition into the Render Queue panel. It opens the Render Queue panel with the Car 3 composition as a render item.

3. Click the **Output to: Not yes specified** link for Output Module. It opens the Output Movie To dialog box on the screen.

4. **Navigate** to a folder to save the rendered output file. In our case, we select Used Images folder of our hard drive.

5. **Type** a name for the output file. In our case, we type: Car Final Composition. By default, the output file is with the name of the composition. Then click the **Save** button.

6. In the Render Queue panel, you can **expand** Render Settings and Output Module by clicking the arrow head to the left of their names to ensure the current settings suit the required output.

By default, the render item is set to output the highest quality. The built-in output templates provide a suitable base for producing an output file complying with the established broadcast video standards. In our case, we go ahead with the default settings.

7. Click the **Render** button which is at the top-right side of the Render Queue panel. Depending on the RAM of your workstation (computer), it will produce the output video file in your selected folder.

Usually, the final composition includes many effects and animation presets with several complex settings. When you render the composition, the rendering process takes several minutes or even hours depending on various factors, such as the composition's settings, size, quality, and compression method used to encode a movie. A progress bar appears in the Render Queue panel showing the progress of the rendering process. After the rendering process is completed, it saves the movie file in the specified location.

Adjusting the Render Settings

Render settings determine how a composition is rendered in After Effects and only affect the output of the render item. By default, the render settings for a render item are based on the current project and composition settings. For instance, if the composition size is 1280 x 720, the default size for the render setting is set as 1280 x 720. By default, the Best Settings template is selected when you add a composition to the render queue. To select a template, click the down arrow head button next to the Render Settings label. A dropdown list appears with the templates.

You can see on your screen that the templates or the pre-defined settings include Best Settings, Current Settings, DV Settings, Draft Settings, Multi-Machine Settings, and Custom. These templates can be of good help; however, for more specific rendering needs, you must modify the individual settings. The Custom option allows you to set the individual settings using the Render Settings dialog box. Alternatively, you can open the Render Settings dialog box by clicking the underlined text, Best Settings. You can also create a new template with the custom render settings using the Make Template option from the dropdown list. The Render Settings Templates dialog box appears where you can specify various settings for the template. These settings are used when you render movies, individual frames, pre-rendered movies, or proxies. Keep in mind that changes to an existing template do not affect render items that are already in the render queue. Perform the following steps to adjust the render settings:

1. **Add** a composition into the Render Queue panel using the **Add to Render Queue** command. In our case, we add the Car 3 composition.

2. Click the underlined text **Best Settings**. In the Render Queue panel, the underlined text functions as buttons. For instance, you can click the Best Settings underlined text to open the Render Settings dialog box. After you click, the Render Settings dialog box appears.

There are several settings in the Render Settings dialog box that are mostly used with their default values. The two most important properties in the Time Sampling section to be adjusted are Field Rendering and Time Span. The Field Render property allows you to switch from progressive to interlaced rendering; whereas, the Time Span property allows you to control the part of the rendered timeline. You can specify either the entire timeline or an area defined by the work area bar, or set custom In Point and Out Point for the composition. It is important to know that progressive and interlaced are two methods of displaying images on a video screen.

3. Click the **Custom** button located in the Time Sampling section to change the default time span. In our case, the composition ends at the 42:25 seconds mark on the Timeline panel. The Custom Time Span dialog box appears on the screen.

4. **Type** 0:00:30:00 in the Duration text box. This changes the End frame to 29.28 seconds (0:00:29:28). In our case, the start time is set to its default (0:00:00:00) as shown in the Start text box. When you set the duration, the end time is automatically set and vice versa, according to the frame rate, which in our case is 29.986 fps (frames per second).

5. Click the **OK** button to close the Custom Time Span dialog box and return to the Render Settings dialog box, which appears with the new duration settings.

6. **Ensure** the Field Render property is set to Off. This default option is primarily used while rendering for film or for display on a computer screen.

7. Click the **OK** button in the Render Settings dialog box to close it with the remaining default settings. The Best Settings underlined text changes to Custom: "Best Settings".

8. Click the **Lossless** underlined text to the right of the Output Module label. By default, Output Module is set to Lossless, which produces a high quality video file. This opens the Output Module Settings dialog box with Main Options tab active.

9. Select the **QuickTime** option from the Format dropdown list to select the output format as QuickTime. The default option is AVI. Then click the **OK** button to close the dialog box.

In the Output Module Settings dialog box, you can also adjust the audio output settings as well as the size of the output video by resizing or cropping it. The Resize, Crop, and Audio Output sections are disabled by default. The Lossless underlined text changes to Custom: QuickTime.

10. Click the **Render** button in the Render Queue dialog box to render the composition with the modified settings. Once the rendering is completed, the status changes to Done in the panel. Now you can play the rendered file (Car Final Composition.mov) from the saved location.

Rendering an Individual Frame

For testing the quality of the output movie, rendering the entire movie is time consuming. Instead, you can render an individual frame as a still image and use it as a visual guide for checking the effects and the overall quality. The rendered frame can also be used for creating freeze-frame effect, where a single frame is paused for specified time duration. In addition, you can use the rendered frame as a thumbnail or preview image.

You can render the frame either as an Adobe Photoshop (PSD) file with layers or a still image. The Photoshop Layers command allows you to save a PSD file that preserves all the layers of a composition. You can save nested compositions in the PSD file as layer groups. The color depth of the PSD file is inherited from the After Effects project. In addition, the layered Photoshop file contains an embedded composite (flattened) image of all the layers. This feature ensures that the file is compatible with applications that do not support Photoshop layers. Here are the steps to render an individual frame:

1. **Activate** the composition from which you want to render an individual frame. In our case, we select the Car 3 composition.

2. **Move** the playhead to any frame that you want to render. In our case, we move to the 34 seconds and 15 frame (0:00:34:15) mark.

You can also manually drag the playhead to the time mark, or click Current Time and type a value in the Current Time text box, and press the Enter key to change the playhead position.

3. Choose **Composition> Save Frame As> File** from the Menu bar. The Render Queue panel appears with the Car 3 composition.

You can see on your screen that the Render Settings option is set to Current Settings, as you selected the Save Frame As command. The Current Settings option outputs the file as a single frame. By default, the Output Module renders an individual frame to a Photoshop file; however, you can change it by editing the module settings.

4. Click the underlined text **Photoshop** to the right of the Output Module label. The Output Module Settings dialog box appears.

5. Select the **JPEG Sequence** option from the Format dropdown list. The JPEG Options dialog box appears on the screen.

6. Select the **Maximum** option in the Quality dropdown list. Then click the **OK** button to close the JPEG Options dialog box. And then, click the **OK** button in the Output Module Settings dialog box.

7. **Click** the underlined text Car 3 (0-00-34-15).jpg next to the Output To label. The Output Frame To dialog box appears.

8. **Select** a location (Used Images) on the hard disk drive to save the still image. Then **type** a name (Car at 3415) in the File name combo box. And then, click the **Save** button to save the file. The Render Queue panel displays the modified settings.

9. Click the **Render** button in the Render Queue panel to render the file. This may take a few minutes; once the rendering is complete, you can edit the file in an image editing software, such as Photoshop.

Duplicating a Render Item

As discussed earlier, you cannot re-render a render item in After Effects. In such case, you can duplicate the render item to create a new render item in the queue with the same or new settings. When you duplicate, all the settings of the original render item are transferred to its copy by default. You can also render the duplicate copy with different settings. For instance, where one format requires interlacing and another requires progressive display; it is necessary to duplicate entire item to make these changes.

To duplicate a render item, select the rendered item and then select Edit> Duplicate from the Menu bar. After duplicating, use the Render Queue panel to specify different settings. However, instead of adding the render item to the Render Queue panel multiple times, you can just assign multiple Output Modules to the item. Perform the following steps to duplicate a render item:

1. **Select** a render item in the Render Queue panel that you want to duplicate. In our case, we select Signatures 2 item.

2. Choose **Edit> Duplicate** from the Menu bar to make a copy of the selected render item. Alternatively, press the Ctrl+D keys together to duplicate the selected render item. A copy of Signature 2 render item appears in the Render Queue panel.

You can also right-click the render item in the Render Queue panel, and select the Duplicate option from the context menu. To replace the original render item, select the Edit> Duplicate with the File Name command from the Menu bar.

After duplicating a render item, you can modify settings for the duplicate copy separately. In case you want to change only the Output Module, you can click the plus button for the Output Module and change the settings separately.

Lesson 20
Trimming a Composition

While creating a composition, using the Composition Settings dialog box, you can specify the dimension and duration for the composition. You may later need to change the composition settings when you need to change the project settings or length of the animation. In such cases, you need to trim the duration of the composition to fit the new specification. In this section, you learn to trim a composition's duration to eliminate extra portion. You can trim the area of a composition defined by the work area bar in the Timeline panel. Perform the following steps to trim a composition:

1. **Select** a composition that you want that you want to trim. In our case, we have opened Custom Text Animation in the Timeline, which includes a typewriter animation.

2. Select **Composition> Composition Settings** from the Menu bar. The Composition Settings dialog box appears with the current composition settings.

You can see on your screen that the selected composition has duration of 2 minutes (0:01:59:28) and the dimension is HDV/HDTV 720 29.97 size of 1280 px x 720 px. However, the typewriter animation effect only lasts for the first 37 seconds and 15 frames. Therefore, we need to trim the composition duration to 45 seconds.

3. Click **OK** button to close the Composition Settings dialog box. Then, **select** the animated text layers in Timeline panel. In our case, we select two animated layers: **Old Mumbai street** and **Shape Layer 1**.

4. **Press** the U key to reveal only the animated properties of the selected layers. The animated properties with keyframes appear on the screen.

You can see on your screen that the animation ends before the 45 seconds mark in the time ruler. In our case, we want to trim the animation to 45 seconds with few extra seconds after the animation ends. These extra seconds at the start and end of the animation is known as handles. Adding few seconds extra at the end of the animation, provides viewers time to register the visuals on screen. In addition, if you plan to import the animation into a video editing application, such as Premiere Pro, this extra space after the animation helps to integrate the animation into another project.

5. **Click** Current Time in the Timeline panel. Then **type** 4500 in the temporarily active text box, and press the **Enter key**. Alternatively, you can type 0:00:45:00 and press Enter key to move the playhead to 45 seconds mark in the timeline.

6. **Press** the N key to move the <u>Work Area End</u> Marker (▯) to the current playhead location. In our case, the Work Area End marker moves to the 45 seconds mark.

Press the B key on the keyboard to move the start of the work area bar to the playhead. Alternatively, hold the Shift key down and drag the Work Area End marker towards the playhead to move the marker towards the playhead. Hold the Shift key down to snap the marker to the playhead.

7. **Right-click** on the <u>Work Area</u> bar and select the **Trim Comp to Work Area** option from the context menu. The Work Area bar is readjusted in the timeline and the total duration of the composition becomes 45 seconds. The Trim Comp to Work Area option trims the duration of the composition to include the area defined by the work area.

Cropping a Composition

Cropping refers to changing the actual dimension of a composition. To suit certain requirements, you may need to crop a composition. The Crop Comp to Region of Interest command allows you to crop the composition to a defined area. You can define the area using the Region of Interest option that is available as a button at the bottom of the Composition panel. Technically, cropping does not delete the area outside the region of interest. It adjusts the composition size so that the excluded area is not displayed. Hence, you can still move the background layer to show the hidden areas. The Region of Interest option helps to preview only a portion of a composition, as only the area inside it is rendered. Reducing the dimension of a composition while resizing it has no impact; however, increasing its dimension results in loss of quality. Perform the following steps to crop a composition:

1. Click the **Choose grid and guide options** (▦) button at the bottom of the Composition panel to crop the composition. A dropdown list appears on the screen.

2. Select the **Proportional Grid** option from the dropdown list. The grid appears in the Composition panel; use this grid to position the content. You can show only one set of grids at a particular time; therefore, when you enable the Proportional Grid option, the Title/Action Safe option is disabled.

3. Click the **Region of Interest** (▭) button at the bottom of the Composition panel. This changes the cursor into a cross-hair icon and disables the layer display. Hence, it is important to set up either the grid or guides in advance.

4. **Click** and **drag** in the Composition panel to define the area that you want to keep. You can see on your screen that the unselected portion fills with black. You can also adjust the region of interest using he handles. In case you want to remove the region of interest, hold the Alt key down and click the Region of Interest button again.

5. Select **Composition> Crop Comp to Region of Interest** from the Menu bar. The composition dimensions are changed to fit the size defined by the region of interest and the excluded portion is removed. You can check the cropped composition settings in the Composition Settings dialog box of your screen.

6. Click the **Choose grid and guide options** button again at the bottom of the Composition panel to crop the composition. A dropdown list appears.

7. Select the **Proportional Grid** option from the dropdown list to disable it. This hides the grid from the Composition panel.

8. Choose Composition> Composition Settings from the Menu bar to open the Composition Settings dialog box. Now you can see on your screen that after cropping, the Width is 1264 px and the Height is 577 px (which was 1280 px x 720 px, earlier).

Exporting in After Effects CS6

After Effects workflow can utilize external software to develop content for online or digital devices. For instance, you can create motion graphics in After Effects, and then export the project to Flash Professional to include interactivity. Technically, exporting is different from rendering. Exporting allows you to recreate an After Effects project and composition in any other software, such as Premiere Pro and Flash Professional. Using the Export command under the File menu, you can export After Effects projects and compositions. In contrast, the Render Queue panel primarily serves as the main interface for rendering or outputting a composition.

You can export a project in different categories, such as video, video project formats, still images formats, and audio. By default, all image file formats are exported at 8 bits per channel (bpc). You can also export data by installing plug-ins or scripts provided by third-parties. To create an animated GIF movie, first render and export a QuickTime movie, and then, import the QuickTime movie in Photoshop; from here, you can export the movie as an animated GIF file using the Save For Web & Devices command. The list below shows various file formats that you can export from After Effects CS6.

Different File Formats to Export

Category	Formats
Video formats	3GPP (3GP), FLV, F4V, H.264, H.264 Blu-ray, MPEG-2, MPEG-2 DVD, MPEG-2 Blu-ray, MPEG-4, QuickTime (MOV), and SWF
Video for Windows	AVI and Windows Media (Windows only)
Video project formats	PRPROJ (Adobe Premiere Pro project) and XFL (Flash Professional)
Still-image formats	Photoshop (PSD; 8, 16, and 32 bpc), Bitmap (BMP, RLE), Cineon (CIN, DPX; 16 bpc and 32 bpc converted to 10 bpc), Maya IFF, (IFF; 16 bpc), JPEG (JPG, JPE), OpenEXR (EXR), PNG (PNG; 16 bpc), Radiance (HDR, RGBE, XYZE), SGI (SGI, BW, RGB, 16 bpc), Targa (TGA, VBA, ICB, VST), and TIFF (TIFF; 8, 16, and 32 bpc)
Audio-only formats	AIFF, MP3, and WAV

Exporting a Project File

After Effects allows you to export native After Effects projects to other Adobe software, such as Premiere Pro and Flash Professional. In addition, you can export an After Effects composition as a Premiere Pro project. You can also copy and paste between After Effects and Premiere Pro or use Dynamic Link to exchange data between these two software. You can also import Premiere Pro projects and sequences into an After Effects project.

If Flash is the intended destination, you can use the Export command to create an Adobe Flash Professional (.xlf) project file. An .xlf file is essentially and XML-based equivalent of the native Flash project file (.fla). When you export a composition to .xfl format, the program preserves maximum data while maintaining the integrity of individual layers and keyframes. However, the .xfl format does not support all layers and effects. After Effects allows you to either rasterize or ignore any layers with unsupported features. Perform the following steps to export a project file into Flash Professional:

1. **Open** an After Effects project that you want to export into Flash Professional. In our case, we open the Text.aep project.

2. Double-click the **Custom Text Animation** composition in the Project panel to make it active in the Timeline panel.

3. Choose **File> Export> Adobe Flash Professional (XFL)** from the Menu bar. By the way, to export the project as a Premiere Pro project, select the Adobe Premiere Pro Project option. It opens the Adobe Flash Professional (XFL) Settings dialog box.

You can see on your screen that this dialog box allows you to select an option for the layers with unsupported features. In the Layers with Unsupported Features section, the Format is set to FLV by default. This format is used to render the layers with unsupported features. You can rasterize layers with unsupported features into Flash Video (FLV) or Portable Network Graphics (PNG) sequence. Keep in mind that layers with supported file types and properties will be handled natively in Flash.

4. Click the **OK** button on the Settings dialog box. It opens the <u>Save As</u> dialog box on the screen. Then **navigate** to any location (Used Images) to save the file. And then, click the **Save** button to save the file and close the dialog box.

By default, the filename takes the composition name. In our case, the default composition name is used with .xfl extension in the File name combo box. The export operation does not affect the project file; hence, you can ignore saving the project in After Effects. The Exporting "Custom Text Animation.xfl" message box appears showing the progress of the export operation.

The file is now ready to be opened in Adobe Flash. When you export an After Effects project as a Premiere Pro project, Premiere Pro uses the settings of the first composition in the After Effects project for all the subsequent sequences. You can export compositions as SWF files for playback within a Web browser.

Exporting a Composition for the Web

The content created After Effects is used in different mediums. The Web is one of the most popular medium for the content created in After Effects. You can export an individual composition or movie to be used in a website. For instance, you can animate a logo in After Effects and export the animated logo to be used in the company's website. For this, you need to render and export the composition as a SWF (Shock Wave File) file. The SWF format is widely used as vector graphics and animation format for the Web that can also contain audio. It is compact and uses binary codes. Any web browser with the Adobe Flash Player plug-in can play a file in this format. Perform the following steps to export a composition for the Web:

1. **Select** a composition that you want to export for the Web. In our case, we select the Custom Text Animation composition.

2. Choose **Composition> Composition Settings** from the Menu bar or press the Ctrl+K keys together to open the Composition Settings dialog box. The Composition Settings dialog box appears on the screen.

3. Select the **Web Video, 320 x 240** option from the Preset dropdown list in the Basic tab. When you select a preset, all settings including Width, Height, Aspect Ratio, and Frame Rate are adjusted based on the selected preset.

4. Click the **OK** button on the dialog box. The new Web-appropriate resolution 320 x 240 pixels is applied to the composition.

As a result of the reduction in composition dimension, the animated layers become bigger than the composition. Now, you need to reposition and resize the layers for the new output medium. You may need to adjust the keyframes of the animated layer to fit the animation within the new frame size.

5. **Adjust** the layers to make it visible in the reduced composition frame size. In our case, we have scaled down the background layer using the Scale property. We have also modified the keyframes to finish the animation within the frame size. You can now render and export the composition in SWF format.

6. Choose **File> Export> Adobe Flash Player (SWF)** from the Menu bar with the Custom Text Animation composition selected. It opens the Save As dialog box on the screen.

7. **Navigate** to a location: (Used Images), **type** a file name as: (Custom Text Animation For Web.swf), and click **Save** button to save the file name and close the dialog box. It opens the SWF Settings dialog box.

8. Select the **High** option from the JPEG Quality dropdown list for better quality. Select **Rasterize** option from the Unsupported Features dropdown list. Select the **Audio** check box to enable audio in the final SWF file. Select the **Loop Continuously** check box to loop the animation. And click the **OK** button with rest of the settings to their defaults.

9. After Effects displays a progress bar as it renders the file and exports it to SWF format. Then **open** the folder in which the SWF file is saved.

It also saves a report in Hypertext Markup Language (HTML) in the same folder of the SWF file. After Effects exports text layer to Shockwave Flash (SWF) as vector layers. However, some layer types and layer switches, such as 3D Layers, 3D Cameras, and 3D Lights are not supported.

10. **Double-click** the HTML file to open it in the default Web browser. You can see that the file is played repeatedly as looping is enabled.

You can also preview the SWF file by clicking the link on the page. Keep in mind that SWF files can be played directly by Adobe Flash Player. You can render FLV files that can be published online, but FLV file must be embedded in a SWF file to be played by Adobe Flash Player.

Exporting Compositions for Mobile Devices

Mobile devices such as mobile phones and the Apple iPod have increasingly become an important medium for digital content created using several softwares. They have small screens compressed to other medium, such as computer and television. Before exporting to mobile devices, you can either crop the composition frame size or create a composition fitting the device screen size. Mobile devices also have limited storage and processor power; therefore, the two important considerations before exporting are: file size and data rate. The following tips can be considered while exporting to mobile devices from After Effects:

- Use a lower frame rate, usually between 12 to 24 fps.
- Apply motion-stabilization, noise-reduction, or blur effects.
- Use limited colors as the mobile devices have less color gamut.
- Use fast transitions, such as cuts instead of zooming in and out or using fades and dissolves to make compression easier.

H.264 is a standard for video compression and derived from the MPEG-4 standard. You can also use presets in the Output Module in the Render Queue panel to render in this format. For instance, the H.264 preset allows you to playback the movies in an iPhone. In this section, you will learn to export in the H.264 format. Perform the following steps to export for mobile devices:

1. **Open** the After Effects project and activate the composition that you want to export for mobile devices. In our case, we select the Custom Text Animation composition.

2. Choose **Composition> Add to Render Queue** from the Menu bar. The composition is added into the queue in the Render Queue panel.

3. Click the **Lossless** underlined text for the Output Module. The Output Module Settings dialog box appears on the screen.

4. **Select** the H.264 option from the <u>Format</u> dropdown list. After selecting this option, you need to click the **OK** button at the bottom.

5 Click the **Render** button in the <u>Render Queue</u> panel. With this, we come to the end of this chapter and the end of learning about After Effects.

Niranjan Jha Showman
Trainer, Author, Physician, Entrepreneur, Filmmaker, Activist
Cromosys Corporation
Education and Technology Research Center
www.facebook.com/cromosys
+91-9561450045
Nallasopara (W), Mumbai, India

NIRANJAN JHA SHOWMAN

Founder - Niranjan Jha Showman

Cromosys Publication

Teach
Yourself
German

NIRANJAN JHA SHOWMAN

Cromosys Publication

Teach Yourself French

NIRANJAN JHA SHOWMAN

Cromosys Publication
Teach
Yourself
Spanish
NIRANJAN JHA SHOWMAN

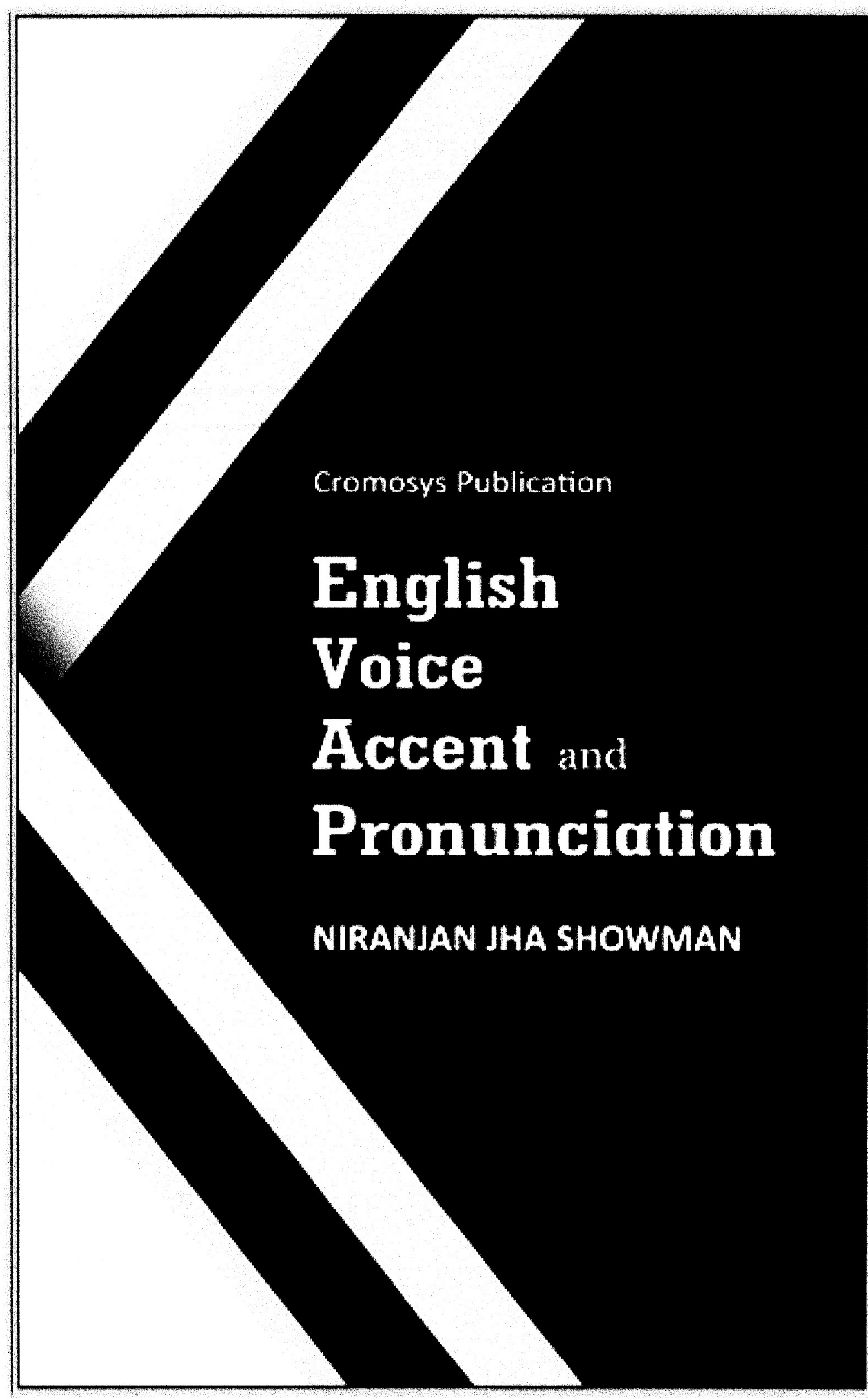

Cromosys Publication

English
Voice
Accent and
Pronunciation

NIRANJAN JHA SHOWMAN

Teach Yourself Autodesk
MAYA

Cromosys Publication

NIRANJAN JHA SHOWMAN

Cromosys Publication
Teach
Yourself
Autodesk
3ds Max
NIRANJAN JHA SHOWMAN

Cromosys Publication
CRIMINAL FACTORY
NIRANJAN JHA SHOWMAN

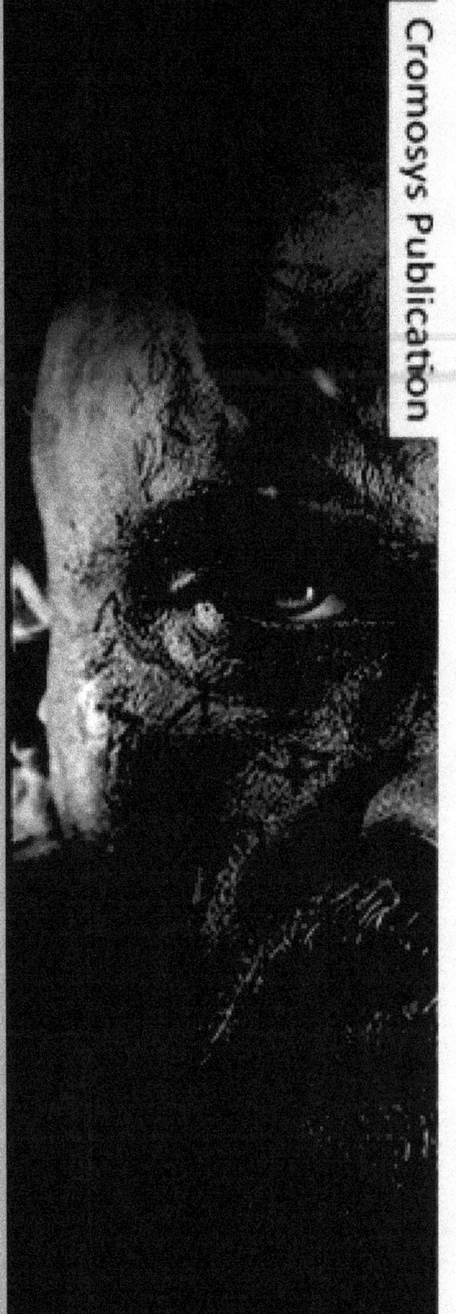

Cromosys Publication
FOCAL DISASTER
NIRANJAN JHA SHOWMAN

Cromosys Publication
Your talents will not help you succeed without your skill of using them.
NIRANJAN JHA SHOWMAN
BE
MILLIONAIRE
LIKE
ME

Copyright Office
Government of India

सत्यमेव जयते

Extracts
from the Register
of Copyrights

Dated : 16/08/2022

1.	Registration Number	:	**T-89782-2022**
2.	Name, address and nationality of the applicant	:	NIRANJAN JHA SHOWMAN, CROMOSYS PUBLICATION, 001, JAYSATYAM, PATANKAR ROAD, NALLASOPARA (W), MUMBA MAHARASHTRA - 401203. INDIAN
3.	Nature of the applicant's interest in the copyright of the work	:	AUTHOR
4.	Class and description of the work	:	LITERARY / BOOK
5.	Title of the work	:	**Teach Yourself Adobe After Effects**
6.	Language of the work	:	ENGLISH
7.	Name, address and nationality of the author and if the author is deceased, date of his decease	:	NIRANJAN JHA SHOWMAN, CROMOSYS PUBLICATION, 001, JAYSATYAM, PATANKAR ROAD, NALLASOPARA (W), MUMBA MAHARASHTRA - 401203. INDIAN
8.	Whether the work is published or unpublished	:	UNPUBLISHED
9.	Year and country of first publication and name, address and nationality of the publisher	:	N.A.
10.	Years and countries of subsequent publications, if any, and names, addresses and nationalities of the publishers	:	N.A. SAME AS ABOVE
11.	Names, addresses and nationalities of the owners of various rights comprising the copyright in the work and the extent of rights held by each, together with particulars of assignments and licences, if any	:	
12.	Names, addresses and nationalities of other persons, if any, authorised to assign or licence of rights comprising the copyright	:	N.A.
13.	If the work is an 'Artistic work', the location of the original work, including name, address and nationality of the person in possession of the work. (In the case of an architectural work, the year of completion of the work should also be shown).	:	N.A.
14.	If the work is an 'Artistic work', whether it is registered under the Designs Act 2000 if yes give details.	:	N.A.
15.	If the work is an 'Artistic work', capable of being registered as a design under the Designs Act 2000.whether it has been applied to an article though an industrial process and ,if yes ,the number of times it is reproduced.	:	N.A.
16.	Remarks, if any	:	

Diary Number :   8723/2020-DF/T
Date of Application :   25/07/2020
Date of Receipt :   25/07/2020

DEPUTY REGISTRAR OF COPYRIGHTS